BEARS

BEARS

Photo by E.H. Baynes/American Museum of Natural History

DONALD DEWEY

GALLERY BOOKS
An Imprint of W.H. Smith Publishers, Inc.
New York, New York 10016

A FRIEDMAN GROUP BOOK

This edition published in 1991 by GALLERY BOOKS
An imprint of W.H. Smith Publishers, Inc.
112 Madison Avenue
New York, New York 10016

ISBN 0-8317-0708-9

BEARS
was prepared and produced by
Michael Friedman Publishing Group, Inc.
15 West 26th Street
New York, New York 10010

Editor: Elizabeth Viscott Sullivan
Art Director: Jeff Batzli
Designer: Susan E. Livingston
Photography Editor: Anne K. Price

GALLERY BOOKS are available for bulk purchase for sales promotions and premium use. For details write or
telephone the Manager of Special Sales, W.H. Smith Publishers, Inc., 112 Madison Avenue, New York,
New York 10016. (212) 532-6600.

Typeset by Bookworks
Color separations by Scantrans Pte. Ltd.
Printed and bound in Singapore by Tien Wah Press Pte. Ltd.

DEDICATION

FOR
ELLEN GOLDENSOHN
FOR BEARING THIS BOOK TO THE AUTHOR

TABLE OF

CONTENTS

INTRODUCTION

Humans have long used animal imagery to characterize ourselves and those around us. We have come to admire the lion for incorporating our sense of superiority, respect the owl for mirroring our wisdom, and wink at the fox for portraying our cleverness. We see our enemies as rats and snakes, our loved ones as kittens and lambs, our stubborn friends as mules. To duck trouble, we know, it is advisable to avoid eager beavers, vultures, shrews and sharks. Hardly a day goes by that we do not encounter a two-legged variation of a goose, skunk, jackal, cow or crab.

Of all the animals charged with human qualities or held accountable for human behavior, none has seduced our imaginations more than the bear. From the astral myths of the ancient Greeks and Asian Indians to the religious rituals of the Finns and Algonquins, from the historical deeds of the Norsemen and Grizzly Adams to the commercial exploits of modern sports franchises, no other animal has equaled the bear as a symbol for human endeavor. In fact, if anthropomorphism is the criterion, the bear, not the dog, has traditionally been our best friend.

Perhaps the most obvious reason for the bear's popularity is its ubiquitousness. At one time or another, some species of bear has roamed over every part of the world, except Australia. Few other creatures have trodden over so much of the planet for so long (the bear's ancestors date back twenty million years). The bear's upright posture and semi-human appearance also seem to have helped earn its distinction: for the ancients, the bear was an apelike reminder of their origins; for all of us, it suggests primitive attributes that we possess to a more or less sophisticated degree. Among the most prominent of these attributes, of course, is ferocity—a quality that must have made a deep impression on the hunter and warrior peoples who once dominated the earth.

One of the most interesting things about our relationship with the bear, however, is that no single characteristic has preemptively defined our perception of the animal. For every representation of the bear typifying strength or ferocity in art, literature and religion, there has been another identifying weakness or cowardice. Depending on the era and culture, the bear has been an embodiment of the devil, an emissary from the gods, a symbol of spring or a reminder to prevent forest fires. The bear has incarnated the seven capital sins and been invoked as a protective spirit for nations and cities. In short, the bear has always conjured up different, even conflicting, imagery and emotions.

This book provides a historical and cultural perspective on the bear and examines the animal as it exists today. *Bears* is intended neither as a scholarly study nor as an exhaustive treatment of its subject: bear lore is far too much fun for the former, and far too massive for the latter. By presenting much of this material collectively, however, I hope to show how the bear occupies one of the largest dens in human imagination.

CHAPTER

1

EARLY
HISTORY

The bear's family tree took root as long as forty million years ago in the Oligocene epoch. The animal's most primal ancestors were miacids, small, tree-climbing carnivores that had canine teeth strong enough to tear into flesh. The miacids also developed a lower-jaw molar and upper-jaw premolar that allowed for the scissoring of flesh into chunks that could be swallowed relatively easily; it was from this latter family of carnivores that dogs, wolves, foxes and bears eventually emerged. Most researchers agree that the first appreciably "bearlike dog" roamed North America twenty-seven million years ago and that the first true bear, a terrier-size mammal called *Ursavus elemensis*, claimed subtropical Europe for a habitat about twenty million years ago. Not until well into the Pliocene epoch, fourteen million years later, did a bear of any significant size emerge.

One of the smallest of the Pliocene bears, *Protursus*, is regarded as the direct sire of the animal we know today. It is something of a marvel that *Protursus* survived to procreate since climactic conditions and other factors in the latter part of the Pliocene epoch caused the extinction of at least nine different bear genera, not to mention a host of species. However, by the time *Protursus* died out, about 2.5 million years ago, near the end of the Pliocene epoch and beginning of the Pleistocene epoch, it had bequeathed to the planet the genus *Ursus*, which included *Ursus minimus*, a small bear that weighed about 100 lbs. and resembled the contemporary sun bear of the Malay Peninsula, Thailand and Borneo. *Ursus minimus* ultimately produced the Etruscan bear *(Ursus etruscus)* that was to populate enormous areas of Europe, Asia and the Americas.

With *Ursus minimus* begins the more detailed history of the bear. It is known, for example, that one of *Ursus minimus*'s descendants crossed Siberian-Alaskan land bridges

THE SPECTACLED BEAR IS THE ONLY BEAR LIVING IN SOUTH AMERICA. IT CAN BE FOUND IN VENEZUELA AND COLOMBIA, IN THE FOOTHILLS OF ECUADOR, PERU AND CHILE, AND SCATTERED ZONES OF BOLIVIA.

into North America at the beginning of the Pleistocene epoch, about 1.5 million years ago, and gradually moved south. The evolution of bears in the new world included a short-faced bear *(Arctodus simus)*, which prowled vast areas of North and South America, and a Florida cave bear *(Tremarctos floridanus)*, which took up residence in a region equivalent in size to the span between Florida and California. The only American survivor from these Ice Age mammals was the spectacled, or Andean, bear of South America. A subsequent migration of Etruscan bear descendants to North America about 250,000 years ago introduced the brown bear to the continent, which led to the evolution of the Alaskan, Kodiak and grizzly bears. The polar bear, *Ursus maritimus*, an offshoot of the brown bear, came into its own about one hundred thousand years ago.

The circumstances surrounding the black bear's arrival in the Americas are less certain, although this bear is generally presumed to have moved there from Asia as another off-

ABOVE: A SUN BEAR. LEFT: A POLAR BEAR.

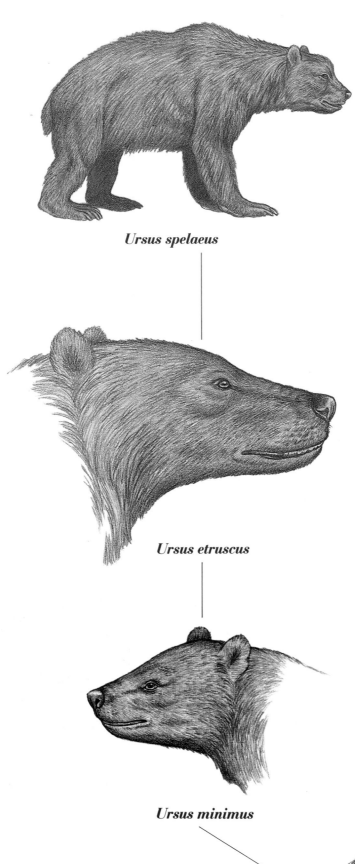

Ursus spelaeus

Ursus etruscus

Ursus minimus

spring of *Ursus etruscus*. What is certain is that both the black bear and the brown bear lived in China and other parts of Asia well before the latter bear's migration to the Americas. Some scholars have not ruled out the possibility that the black bear may have even headed for the Bering Land Bridge before its brown cousin did.

Europe's most conspicuous legacy from the Etruscan bear was the cave bear *(Ursus spelaeus)*, a contemporary of both Neanderthal and Cro-Magnon man. Tens of thousands of cave bear fossils found in Central Europe date back to a period extending from at least fifty thousand (some scholars say two hundred thousand) to ten thousand years ago and suggest a mammal that could have weighed up to 900 lbs.; had a broad, domed skull with some eerily human facial features; and could not have been notably equipped for any accelerated pursuit of prey.

Beyond these points, however, there has been substantial disagreement among paleontologists over both the cave bear's living habits and the reasons for its extinction. Some researchers have even argued that, its genus notwithstanding, the cave bear was a herbivore, not a carnivore. This conjecture has

Ursavus elemensis

been based principally on the vegetable matter found in the stomach remains of the animals and on the frequent incidence of actinomycosis, a debility of the jaw associated with plant eaters. Opponents of this view have observed that the stomachs of even contemporary meat-eating bears contain mostly vegetable matter and have rejected the appearance of the actinomycosis as proof that the fossils under study were found in caves; they believe that older and frailer animals would have inevitably retired to such lairs and that far more numerous healthy specimens would have been the prey of larger mammals or died outdoors for various other reasons.

Although cave bears are so named because of the location of the fossil discoveries, some researchers have interpreted the name more literally and have even attributed this bear's

extinction to its cave dwelling. In particular, these researchers have related the frequency of spinal column and inflammation disorders found in the remains in caves in Switzerland, Austria and Hungary to diseases often contracted by animals confined to cages or other small areas for extended periods. But the majority view is that, Ice Age climactic conditions or not, there is not enough evidence to support speculations that the European bear retreated to caves for more than the usual denning months. As for why the cave bear became extinct relatively quickly, the consensus has been that its meat made it a special object of early man's hunting affections (many cave bear skeletons indicate ax blows) and that it was otherwise the victim of the same conditions that brought about the extinction of so many other mammals in the same era.

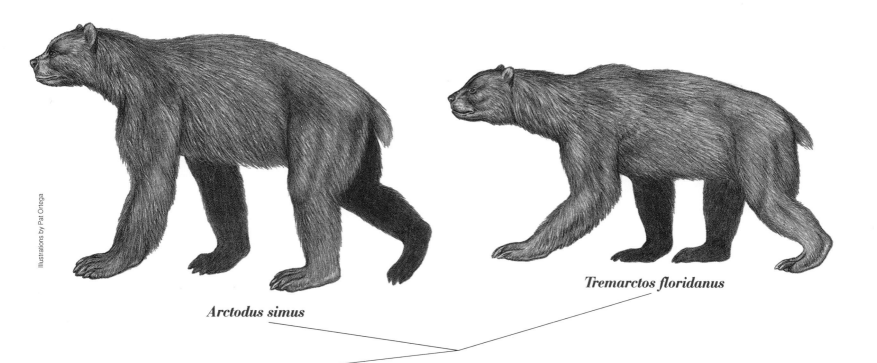

Illustrations by Pat Ortega

Arctodus simus

Tremarctos floridanus

CHAPTER

2

GENERAL
PHYSICAL
ATTRIBUTES
AND HABITS

Overall, bears can be described as coarsely pelted omnivores with thick limbs, short necks and big heads. They have round ears, small eyes and prominent snouts. The bear's average adult weight varies from species to species, from the 100-lbs.-or-so sun bear to the almost-a-ton Kodiak. Bears have curving, non-retractile claws, which are longer on their hind feet than they are on their front feet. Like humans, bears are plantigrade mammals; they place their soles and heels flat on the ground when they walk. This characteristic makes it easy for bears to stand on their hind feet—a posture they adopt when they reach for objects, fight or survey a terrain.

Bears in the wild have been known to live well past thirty years, but this is now more an exception than a rule. Unfortunately, today it is not rare for the entire bear population of a given territory to be less than ten years old because of the depredations of hunters, diseases and combat among the bears themselves.

Human hunters have always been among the bear's most conspicuous enemies, but they are far from being the only ones. Fellow canids such as wolves and wild dogs have tormented the bear for ages—knowledge humans utilize in their traditional use of dog packs for bear hunts. If not daily, bears are frequently the prey of mountain lions and other big cats. The polar bear in particular has natural nemeses in bull walruses and killer whales. Generally, however, neither man's weapons nor other mammals have proven as destructive to the bear as has the steady loss of its territory and attendant food supplies to human settlements.

As a result of centuries of folktales, tall tales and faulty observations, the bear has attracted numerous misconceptions as to its physical abilities and living habits. The most popular of these misconceptions are that the animal is clumsy, has impaired vision and is a loner. However, there is very little evidence to support the first of these claims and plenty of proof to refute the other two. The bear employs its senses to an elaborate degree, and its family is an important part of its life.

A NINETEENTH-CENTURY ENGRAVING OF A BEAR HUNT.

Northwind Picture Archives

© Wolfgang Kaehler

AGILITY
AND SENSES

Because of their generally dogged-looking progress while ambling along on all fours, bears often give the impression of being rather clumsy. However, despite their appearance and the dense layers of fat that lie beneath their pelts, many bears can run like thorough-bred horses; some brown bears have been clocked at 40 mi. an hour—a pace that would enable them to catch a horse. Bears are also generally good climbers and, with an exception or two, they are truly capable swimmers.

The bear's tactile capacity is manifest in its practice of walking within existing footprints. Brown bears, for example, shamble along by setting their hindpaws into the prints their frontpaws make; bears traveling along the same route match the strides. In fact, zoolo-

gists have recorded many cases of hundreds of miles of trails in the snowy countryside that have thousands of superimposed pawprints from successive bears.

The bear's reputation for poor vision seems to stem in part from the animal's singular way of avoiding direct looks at the objects it approaches, and from the hasty but not uncommon conclusion that any creature with exceptional smelling or hearing abilities (which bears have) must suffer limitations in one of the other senses. However, as increasing evidence has suggested in recent decades, bears not only have good eyesight, not to mention particularly developed peripheral vision, but even may be able to distinguish colors. The single fact that the animal actively prowls both day and night already provides a strong argument against any visual handicap.

POLAR BEAR TRACKS IN THE SNOW IN THE CHURCHILL AREA OF MANITOBA, CANADA.

One theory on the bear's seeming reluctance to stare at an object directly is that such a look might connote challenge within the bear kingdom. Over the years, numerous witnesses have reported instances where two bears averted their glances from one another as they inspected a common arena, but would suddenly glower if one felt that the other had approached too closely to its browsing spot. The same phenomenon holds true for people who have ventured too close to the animal as well. Some naturalists believe that many other animals, even those not of the canid family, anticipate danger and react similarly when they feel they are being stared at.

The bear's evasive sightings in the normal course of its wanderings are made all the more possible by a peripheral vision that seems to be second to none in the animal kingdom. One of many typical testimonies on this ability is offered by nature photographer Terry Domico in his book, *Bears of the World:*

> *Bears are very good at detecting movement, even at long distances, as I accidentally learned one morning. For ten days and nights I had been sitting in a rented car watching bear traffic come and go at a municipal dump in northern Canada. My morning watch normally begins at 3:30 A.M. and would continue until about 10:30 A.M., when bear activity would practically cease.*
>
> *One morning I sat there among the buzzing flies, with the window open and my elbow on the sill, my hand gripping the edge of the car's roof where it meets the upper door. Approximately 200 to 300 feet away, eight adult black bears scrounged through the garbage. As I watched, remaining very still, a fly lit on the finger of my hand that was holding onto the roof. I moved the finger to chase it away. Immediately, nearly every bear at the dump lifted its head to look at me. They must have caught the movement in their peripheral vision.*

Many zoologists have compared the bear's sense of smell to that of a dog's. Some observers have reported that the animal can detect a man from a mile away and carrion from as far away as 12 mi. The bear also hears well enough to pick up human conversation from a distance of 300 yds.

Perhaps more noteworthy than the strength of its individual senses is the composite effect of all of the bear's sensitivities. In their book *The Sacred Paw*, Paul Shepard and Barry Sanders describe it this way:

> *When a bear enters a feeding area where other bears are present—a situation pregnant with explosive tension—the new arrival seems almost heedless of the others, regardless of their various sizes and genders, or of the moods that charge the*

atmosphere. Yet it is clear from the path he takes, the adjustments in his behavior and demeanor, and the assertiveness of his feeding that he is aware of every bear around him and all postures, movements, odors, and sounds that signal their intentions. This combination of overall awareness and seeming nonchalance is among the bear's most manlike capacities: a taciturn, calculating mixture of knowing and blasé sophistication that can be unnerving to human observers.

Of course, how "knowing" the bear actually is in terms of intelligence has remained an open question. One sign of the animal's elevated mental capacities, according to researchers, is its inordinate curiosity—not merely about food possibilities, but about any strange or unfamiliar object that it comes across. Hunters have claimed that bears are also adept at covering their tracks when in flight from humans. It also has been reported that bears can even dismantle traps without ensnaring themselves.

SOCIALIZATION

The long-held image of the bear as a social loner has been clouded by more exhaustive scientific observations in recent decades; there now seems to be very little doubt that, as with other animals, its basic social unit is the family, if in a broad sense of the term. Bears spend up to the first thirty-six months of their lives with their mothers and siblings and frequently feed and travel with their brothers and sisters after that. Since females reproduce every two to three years, it is obvious that they are accustomed to having company as well. Adult males are unquestionably more footloose, especially in southern climates, but

© Edwin L. Wright

OPPOSITE PAGE: GRIZZLY BEARS ON A FORAGING EXPEDITION. ABOVE: A POLAR BEAR MOTHER WITH SUCKLING CUBS.

many of them have been sighted staying close to their families. Of more relevance, in the view of many researchers, is the fact that while male adults do not generally demonstrate the tight clan habits of other mammals, they still live their entire lives within growling distance of the families they have sired and the other males in a given territory. As Shepard and Sanders put it:

> *If socialization is defined by living in packs or year-round mate association, then bears are solitary. But perhaps the net of bear sociality is cast so wide that primate observers like men, with their poorer senses of smell and hearing, cannot appreciate its subtlety and scale. If bears have in their heads a constantly revised map of the locations of other individual bears, should we not then consider them as truly socially oriented?*

A POLAR BEAR TAKING THE MEASURE OF AN INTRUDER.

TERRITORIALITY

Even if there persists a question in some minds about the degree of a bear's socialization, there has never been any doubt about the animal's attachment to the footmarks, tree scratchings, urinations, defecations and other bodily excretions that mark its territorial range. Indeed, few animals have the bear's homing instinct. In one celebrated incident in Michigan some years ago, an adult male black bear returned to its native habitat after having been deposited by air a good 150 mi. away. Another experiment in Alaska with a group of brown bears saw them require less than two months to backtrack over a distance of 125 mi. Perhaps one of the most astonishing cases occurred in Alaska in the autumn of 1973 when a young brown bear was moved to Montague Island in Prince William Sound, about 58 mi. from its original territory. Two

months later, the animal was found dead 100 yds. from where it had been captured originally. To have reached that point, the bear had to have swum 7 mi. to one island, another half-mile to a second island, then 2 mi. to the mainland, all the time swimming against the gelid currents of Prince William Sound. In the wake of such episodes, game protection authorities began to reconsider the efficacy of dealing with nuisance bears by removing them to other territories.

The precise extent of a bear's home range varies with its food sources and other factors, not the least of which is the presence of man. Some bears in the United States have been recorded as ranging around an area as large as 250 sq. mi., although this is rare. Determining a mean estimate of the bear's range is more difficult as females normally embrace much smaller areas than males; females sometimes cover only about 20 percent of the male's territory. The overlapping of bear territories is commonplace and is generally regulated by mutual avoidance. During the mating season in early summer, however, aroused males show a preference for fighting rather than wandering away, which can lead to ferocious combats.

Overall, in an area that offers sufficient food and adequate cover, the bear is apt to stay within a smaller zone. On less favorable terrain, the animal has shown a tendency to go along an hourglass route, where it takes in some 50 or 60 sq. mi., its feeding and drinking zones linked to daybed rest stops by corridors that have been traveled repeatedly over the years. The daybeds—for the most part trampled spots in bushes or shallow pits dug

A BLACK BEAR WITH SALMON ON ITS MIND.

© Lee Kuhn/FPG International

into the ground—always provide a command-ing view of the surrounding area.

For all their intelligence and independent spirit, bears can be notoriously captive to the hierarchies established by the physical domi-nance of particular males in a given territory. Some writers have gone so far as to claim that a bear's innate respect for hierarchical order prevents many bloody encounters in ursine society. Other researchers dispute this notion, noting that the numerous scars found on the hide of an average elderly bear indicate a somewhat embattled life.

Not surprisingly, the dominant bears in each population are almost always male and almost always bigger than their fellow bears. The one exception to this gender dominance is a female in the company of her cubs; know-ing the female's readiness to fight to the death for her children, even the most imposing of male leaders tends to leave her alone. Other-wise, the male will assert his position as a matter of course and expect deference. If some would-be usurper attempts to cut ahead of the dominant bear at a salmon stream, for example, the dominant bear will quickly put its challenger in its place with an impatient roar or threatening stare or it will wave an open mouth near its challenger's head (mouthing). Only when the dominant bear has shown signs of age or physical weakening will a challenger persist, ultimately leading to a ritualized combat.

© Gerry Ellis/The Wildlife Collection

HIBERNATION

Do they or don't they? At one time, the question of whether bears hibernated elicited very decisive positive replies. Subsequently, the same question prompted equally decisive negative answers. Most recently, the attitude among researchers has been that bears do not hibernate in the way that, say, bats do, but that their winter denning has enough comparable features to justify using the term *hibernation* in a broad sense.

The bear's retreat to a warm enclosure coincides with the arrival of winterlike weather, although it has remained an open question among some scientists as to whether the true cause of the move is the climate, the shortened day, the scarcer food supply or a combination of these factors. Whatever the immediate motivation for the move, the bear prepares for it for months by consuming up to 20,000 calories a day in order to accumulate sufficient fat reserves and by lining its den with dried grasses and other vegetation for making an insulated bed. The den may be a cave, ground hole, tree hollow or a secluded spot under logs or bushes.

Bears remain in hibernation from two to seven months, the females normally staying longer than the males. During the period the animal will not eat, drink, urinate or defecate. In fact, some species get ready for the winter by feeding on such indigestible materials as resinous plants to block their rectums. The bear is never fully dormant, so it can be awakened fairly easily; on the other hand, if it is not disturbed, it is capable of staying in the same position for a month or more. A bear burns about 4,000 calories a day during hibernation; its body fat drops 20 to 30 percent and provides sustaining food and water through its breakdown. The oxygen supply is maintained to the brain but not to all muscles; estimates are that the overall oxygen consumption drops only by a relatively small 50 percent. A typical bear's heart rate will fall during hibernation from forty to eight beats a minute.

REPRODUCTION

Female bears usually do not mate until they have reached six or seven years of age. Depending on their health, rivals and other normal survival factors, they will then reproduce about every two-and-a-half to three years until they are fifteen. Female bears average three litters in a lifetime.

Bears mate by having the male mount the female from behind. The male will usually wrap its forelimbs around a female's waist to gain greater purchase. Depending on the species, copulation can last from one to twenty minutes. The chief exceptions to this are pandas, whose couplings rarely last more than thirty seconds.

Northern bears give birth during the winter months, while southern species give birth at various times. Like kangaroos, armadillos and some deer, bears are aided in the birth process by a survival mechanism referred to as delayed implantation. This ensures that, while the female may conceive in the broadest sense during a late spring or summer mating, the fertilized egg does not get implanted in the wall of the uterus until well into the autumn months. During the interim months, the cells produced from the growth of a fertilized ovum remain in something of a free float, postponing the embryo's development. Once implantation takes place, the gestation period for the birth of cubs is between six and eight weeks.

Given the brief gestation period, it is not too surprising that cubs are born unusually small; they average no more than 10 to 12 oz., or about $1/700$ of the mother's weight (at birth, human infants weigh about $1/20$ of their mother's weight). Usually the cubs take about forty days to open their eyes, which has prompted the widely held, but only loosely accurate, notion that bears are born blind. After a couple of months of feeding off the mother's high-protein, exceptionally fatty milk, the cubs will weigh about 20 lbs. and take their first steps out of the lair. They spend most of their days foraging, rooting and play-fighting with their siblings under the mother's supervision. For all their antic behavior, however, cubs are extremely aware of the dangers posed to them by adult male bears and stay away from them. In some territories, as much as 40 percent of the cubs will be killed by adult males.

© Irene Vandermolen/FPG International

© Michael H. Francis/The Wildlife Collection

© W. Perry Conway/Tom Stack and Associates

OPPOSITE PAGE: A BABY POLAR BEAR. TOP, LEFT: A BLACK BEAR INFANT. TOP, RIGHT: A THREE-MONTH-OLD GRIZZLY CUB. BOTTOM: A MOTHER GRIZZLY WITH TWO OF ITS OFFSPRING.

A NAPPING SEAL ON THE ICE
NEAR THE WATER IS
FREQUENTLY THE PREY OF
THE POLAR BEAR, WHICH
DEPENDS HEAVILY ON THE
SEAL'S BLUBBER FOR SURVIVAL.

HUNTING AND EATING HABITS

Night or day, bears spend most of their prowling hours on the lookout for food. Only in the case of significant human activity will they restrict their foraging, usually to the twilight hours of the morning and evening.

Although they derive from the miacid family that distinguished itself for developing premolars useful to tear flesh, bears no longer have these teeth, and they depend on pointed canines for killing prey. Their molars are also more typical of herbivores, so it is not surprising that an estimated 75 percent of their diets consists of vegetable matter.

Their omnivorous diets might prompt a conclusion that bears are satisfied to be gourmands, but they often show gourmetlike discrimination. For instance, while plants have always been a staple food, most bears particu-

larly enjoy them in their early flowering stages, when protein content is high. Similarly, a bear used to dining on salmon has tastes that vary with its hunting success: if the bear has not had a good meal for a few days, it will grab any salmon that comes its way and swallow it whole; if, on the other hand, it has been eating regularly, it will become more selective and go only for the nutrition-rich eggs of a female fish. There are many testimonies of Alaskan bears getting their paws on a salmon, discovering that it was a male, and then throwing it away to go after a female.

Allowing for the differences among the species in question, scientists have also detected a general progression in the bear's eating habits. When the animal emerges from its winter den it first grazes on plants, then focuses on fish for a few weeks, moves on to berries and currants, and finally, depending on its availability, concentrates on the meat of other mammals. Interspersed with all these stages, bears also scavenge around garbage dumps and campsites.

The bear's hunting techniques depend on the terrain and the prey. Both brown and black bears, in quest of reindeer or some other large game, stalk very much like cats, then suddenly leap forward and bring down their objective with forepaw blows and neck bites. The extremely wily polar bear accosts seals on floes by slithering across the ice on its stomach, covering its black nose with its paws whenever the prey looks in its direction, then making a final dash toward its victim. Grizzlies will excavate mounds of dirt to get at a squirrel, badger or other creature that it has put on the menu.

Bears attract a host of internal and external parasites. Of the sixty-odd pests that have been identified as being bear parasites, the most dangerous to both the animal and to anyone with a taste for bear meat is the roundworm *Trichinella*, which causes the feverish illness trichinosis. Almost all polar bears and a majority of brown bears become infected with *Trichinella*, which reproduces in the stomach and dispatches larvae throughout the bloodstream of a human or animal host, often with fatal consequences. The only effective human defense against a trichinosis attack is a thorough cooking of all bear meat.

THE BLACK BEAR MAKES ITS CATCH.

© Thomas Kitchen/Tom Stack and Associates

DISTRIBUTION

There are eight species of bear in the world, and they are distributed among the following places:

Brown bear: Europe, Asia and North America

Polar bear: Soviet Union, Norway, Greenland, the United States and Canada

American black bear: Canada, the United States and northern Mexico

Moon bear: Himalayas, most of Asia

Sun bear: India, Malaysia, Thailand and Indonesia

Sloth bear: Sri Lanka, India and Nepal

Spectacled bear: South America

Giant panda: China

With the exceptions of the American black bear and polar bear, all the species have been faced with increasingly grave threats to their existence in recent decades. The main cause of the extinction danger has been our relentless advance into the animal's habitats. The moon bear and the panda are considered particularly endangered. Although individual governments and international organizations have undertaken projects for protecting the bear, they have represented relatively insignificant defenses against deforestation, expanded agriculture areas, hunting, poaching, trafficking in bear parts and other causes of the bear's demise around the world. Even the relatively safe American black bear (an estimated population of 450,000 makes it more numerous than all the other species together) has been disappearing from many states, raising a long-range specter of forced inbreeding that will also ultimately prove fatal to the genus.

One conservation tactic that appears not to have worked is the creation of special game reserves. According to many experts, such areas, no matter how well policed, ultimately make it easier for determined poachers to get to the animals. Some researchers believe that the only long-range tactic that will help the bear's survival is convincing society that our and the bear's survival is linked to the preservation of forest resources. In the words of Dr. Christopher Servheen of the United States Fish and Wildlife Service: "What is good resource use for bear conservation is also good resource use for human survival and quality of life."

TOP: A GIANT PANDA. MIDDLE:
A GRIZZLY COUNTENANCE.
LEFT: THE SPECTACLED BEAR
OF SOUTH AMERICA.

CHAPTER

3

THE BEAR IN
MYTHOLOGY

The bear is perhaps the world's most popular mythological animal. Reflecting its physical presence on every continent except Australia, the bear has been at the center of religious beliefs and rituals from Scandinavia to Chile, from Japan to Mexico and from Canada to Africa. In one culture or another, at one time or another, the bear has represented a god or devil, star or earth and the origin or destiny of humans.

One of the main reasons for the bear's dominance in the human imagination is its decidedly cyclical behavior. Few other creatures could have been as suggestive to primitive humans as this shaggy animal that went to ground with the onset of winter, stayed "buried" there through the cold months, reemerged in spring with new cubs, pursued most of its activities in warm or mild weather and began gathering food again in time for another winter. In its seasonal patterns, the bear was a living metaphor for all the fears, wonders and mysteries of human existence. In retrospect at least, it seems inevitable that such a fundamental and ambivalent relationship encouraged every exorcising and sanctifying power that ritual could offer for making known our reliance on, and earnest intentions toward, the animal.

ASTRAL MYTHS

The most significant argument among the world's mythologies on the bear focuses on the question of whether the heavens first sent the bear to humans or whether a real bear was drafted from earth to set into the firmament. Otherwise Eastern and Western mythologies have been strikingly similar in their depiction of the bear as a contemporary of the gods that deserves veneration; this belief held particularly true with regard to the astral origins of Ursa Major and Ursa Minor.

The most familiar Western astral myth is undoubtedly the Greek story about the huntress-goddess Artemis and her companion Kallisto. As the tale goes, Zeus seduced the pure Kallisto and impregnated her. When

THIS CELESTIAL MAP SHOWS THE CONSTELLATIONS OF THE GREAT BEAR (URSA MAJOR) AND THE LITTLE BEAR (URSA MINOR), WHOSE ORIGINS ARE EXPLAINED BY THE GREEK MYTH OF KALLISTO AND ARTEMIS.

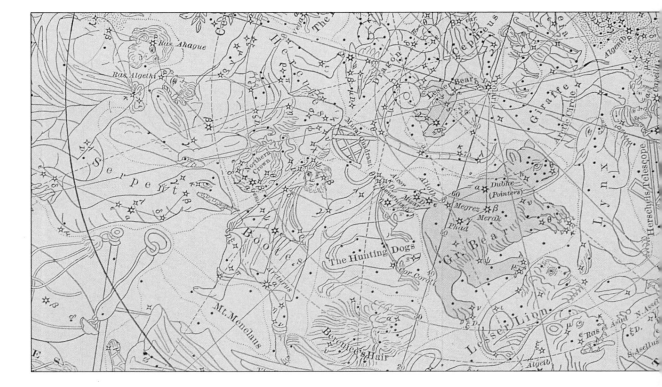

Hera, Zeus's consort, learned that Kallisto was about to deliver her husband's child, she changed the girl into a bear and deceived the huntress Artemis into killing the bear as she would have any other beast of the forest. Hearing of Kallisto's death, Zeus set her among the constellations as the Great Bear (Ursa Major) and also saw to it that her delivered son was spirited away to be raised on Mount Kyllene under the name of Arkas. But the vindictive Hera wasn't through: when she discovered that Kallisto had been placed among the constellations, she fixed it so that the Great Bear would revolve ceaselessly around the Pole Star, never to be permitted to bathe in the pure waters of Okeanos.

One of several variations on this tale identifies Artemis and Kallisto as the same character and has Hera slaying the transformed maiden. Almost all the versions trace the creation of the Little Bear (Ursa Minor) to the later death of Arkas and Zeus's decision to have the son serve as his mother's eternal guardian.

This myth is repeated, with alterations, in other folklore as well. The Romans had a

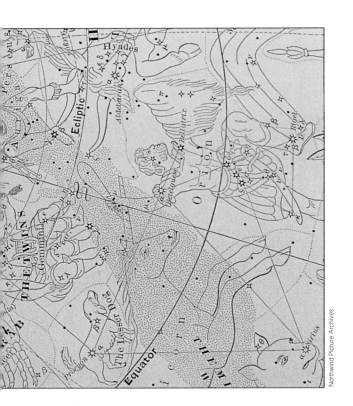

Northwind Picture Archives

New York Public Library Picture Collection

similar story about the creation of Ursa Major and Ursa Minor, with the huntress Diana replacing Artemis. The Celtic goddess Artio also seems to be a mythological descendant of Artemis. In their mythology, the Hindus went one step further than the Greeks in making the Great Bear the source of all universal energy and referring to the seven visible stars of Ursa Major as the Seven Rishis (sages). In his book *Omens and Superstitions of Southern India*, Edgar Thurston wrote that the Hindus held that the constellation caused "seasons to follow one another in regular succession, rains to fall, and crops to grow and ripen. . . . It assured a supply of food. But if it provided health and strength, it also, as the controller of water and wind, brought about droughts in season, and sent blights and diseases on evil winds."

Allowing for the different perceptions of the number of stars in Ursa Major because of latitude factors, compare the description of the Hindu belief with an Algonquin myth reported in *The Journal of American Folklore:*

© Charles Mann

*The bear was trying to escape from a
hunter who followed him until the middle
of September. . . . A chickadee with a kettle
or dipper on his back was keeping close
behind the hunter. When the hunter over-
took the bear, he put an arrow through
the bear's heart. As the blood flowed
from the bear's side, the chickadee filled
his dipper until the blood overflowed,
and when it fell to the earth it reddened
the leaves as we now see them in autumn.
The white grease then dripping from the
bear's body became snow upon the
earth—whence winter.*

Numerous other Indian peoples throughout
North America have similar myths about the
effect of the bear on the seasons. For the
Ostyaks and other Siberian peoples, on the
other hand, the emphasis was on the bear's
decision to descend from its heavenly home
to mingle with humans. One of the more
noted Ostyak stories depicts the bear as having been content to live on a cloud near the
already-existing Great Bear constellation until
the day a cub known as Little Bear acciden-
tally put its paw through the clouds, saw the
humans below and begged to be allowed to
go down and play with them. It was during
Little Bear's visit that men were taught the
importance of honoring the bear. When Little
Bear had to return to the heavens, it filled its
knapsack with silver objects given in tribute;
these objects ultimately accounted for the
shining lights of the constellation.

For the Ostyaks, as for the Finns and several other peoples, the bear was very much of
heavenly issue, arising from "the lands between the sun and the moon" and ultimately
dying "not at the hands of men, but of its
own will." So venerated was the animal, especially among Finno-Ugric and Siberian peoples, that it was considered blasphemous,
even dangerous, to refer to it explicitly by
name. Thus the Finns called the bear "honey
paw" or "the great forest," while the Ostyaks
denoted it as "the fur man" and "the dweller
in the wild." Even more creative were Europe's Lapps, who had a storehouse of epi-
thets, including "master of the forest," "holy
animal," "old man of the mountains," "dog
of God" and "the wise one."

Armenians and Eskimos are among the
numerous peoples who disagree with the
Finns and the Ostyaks, but instead believe
that the bear was raised into heaven after an
earthly existence. One typical Eskimo story
describes a woman who happens across a
family of bears in human form and settles
down with them for a while. Eventually, however, she confesses that she misses her husband and asks the bears to allow her to return
home. The bears agree, but only on the con-

dition that she not reveal the location of their dwelling to her husband. The woman does tell her husband, who goes to the dwelling. The bears are enraged, and one of them goes to the woman's home, gives her a mortal bite on the neck, and is about to escape when it is set upon by the husband's dogs. Suddenly, in the middle of a fierce battle between the bear and the dogs, a great fire descends from the sky, engulfs them and returns them to the sky as Ursa Major.

CREATION MYTHS

Astral myths hardly exhaust man's earliest perceptions of the bear. The animal also figures prominently in various creation myths, and usually in a way that makes it clear that even the gods took on more than they were able to handle. Consider this tale of the origins of the animal kingdom as it is recounted by the Shasta Indians in Ella Clark's *Indian Legends of the Pacific Northwest*:

> *When Manitou the Great Spirit had wandered long enough on earth, he was resolved to fill it with animals. He took his long staff, broke off a piece at the bottom, rubbed it to splinters, and then threw them into the water. Out of these came the fishes. Then he pulled a few leaves from the trees, held them in the hollow of his hand, and blew them into the air. They became birds. The middle of his staff he broke into big and small pieces, and they ran, hopped, and crawled away as animals. Finally, there remained only the stout, rounded end that he had kept in his hand until then, and he turned it into a creature stronger and cleverer than all the other creatures. This was the grizzly bear, so strong and so fierce that Manitou himself quickly had to flee from it and take refuge on the top of Mount Shasta. In those days the grizzlies still walked erect as men did later, and they did not kill their prey with teeth and claws, but with clubs.*

For the Gypsies, the bear was created to provide them with their traditional livelihood by divine intervention. As one ancient tale goes, a Gypsy girl awoke one morning to discover that she was pregnant despite her virginity. Horrified by her predicament, the girl

The University Museum, University of Pennsylvania

THIS BEARCLAW HEADDRESS WAS MADE BY THE TLINGIT TRIBE OF SOUTHEAST ALASKA, AND WAS WORN BY SHAMANS CURING VICTIMS OF ILLNESS BY WITCHCRAFT. THE SHAMAN WOULD TOUCH THE CLAWS TO THE PATIENT'S BODY TO HEAL HIM OR HER. THE SOUND OF THE CLAWS RATTLING TOGETHER SUPPOSEDLY SUMMONED THE SPIRITS TO HELP THE SHAMAN PERFORM HIS CURE.

Northwind Picture Archives

**PERFORMING BEARS HAVE
BEEN A STAPLE OF SMALLTOWN
LIFE IN EASTERN EUROPE FOR
CENTURIES.**

decided to drown herself in a nearby lake. Just as she was about to do herself in, a spirit rose out of the water and told her not to be ashamed, that she would give birth to a divinely protected creature capable of working like a man. The issue turned out to be a bear that was immediately adopted by the girl's entire tribe and taught to dance and perform tricks. This story has become particularly associated with the *Ursuari*, the "bear exhibitors" of the Balkans who have made their living for centuries by training the animal to perform in carnivals and circuses.

HEROIC MYTHS

Norse and Teutonic mythology is filled with stories that attest to the bear's divine nature or preternatural powers. One such tradition concerns the *Fylgja*, guardian spirits that could detach themselves from the bodies of human beings and make themselves visible in an animal form appropriate to the personality of their owners (foxes for cleverness, birds for grace and so on). Of all the animal forms assumed by the *Fylgja*, the bear was considered to be the most prestigious, as it was associated exclusively with great warriors and chieftains. One such warrior was the Danish hero Bothvar Bjarki, who once slept through the initial hours of an important battle. When he finally roused himself and hurried down to the fighting, he was assured that he hadn't been missed, that his bear-*Fylgja* had stood in for him valiantly and had gone away only when it saw him arrive.

In a lighter vein, there is the story of a young boy, Thorsten, who stumbled as he ran into a room to see his grandfather. The old man laughed and said that Thorsten didn't see the bear cub–*Fylgja* playing in front of

the door. With a bear as his guardian spirit, of course Thorsten grew up to become an honored warrior.

Two other bearlike characters figure conspicuously in the mythology of Northern Europe. Like its wolf counterpart in the legends of Southern and Central Europe, Northern Europe's werebear was a tormented creature that had to satisfy its darkest urges by attacking other animals and men. Unlike the werewolf, however, the werebear prowled only during the day, and the sun played the same role in its curse as the full moon did in the legends in other parts of the Continent. In a few of the werebear tales, the curse is brought down on the hero by a stepmother, a character that many commentators have linked to the role played by Hera in the Greek myths about Arkas and his natural mother, Kallisto.

The second important Northern European figure was the Berserker, a warrior who went into battle covered in nothing more than a bearskin, but whose ursine frenzy and daring made him practically invulnerable to enemy weapons. Although mortal, the Berserker was believed to enjoy extra protection from Odin, so that he usually fell in battle only after many years of combat. A typical description of these fierce warriors is found in the *Ynglinga Saga*:

> . . . *[Odin's] men went without mailcoats, and were frantic as dogs or wolves; they bit their shields and were as strong as bears or boars; they slew men, but neither fire nor iron could hurt them. This is known among men as "running berserk."*

By giving select warriors special power on the battlefield, Odin made it impossible for

GEORGE CATLIN'S PAINTING,
BEAR DANCE, PREPARING FOR A BEAR HUNT, 1835–37.

them to live normally, even within their own families. The Icelandic poet Egill Skallagrims-son recorded, for instance, how his Berserker father once became so overwrought during a game with him that he killed the child's nurse and almost tore him apart as well. Similar tales exist in many neighboring countries, such as Norway, Denmark and Sweden. Rather than being able to live within normal society, the consensus of the tale suggests, Berserkers were doomed to go from battle to battle until they found an enemy more ferocious than themselves.

While Berserkers have generally been identified with the Vikings of the ninth century, they were in fact a part of a long tradition of Northern European shock troops said to have borrowed their savagery from the animal king-dom. As far back as the first century, the Roman historian Tacitus had described similar warriors among such Germanic tribes as the Chatti, Harii and Heruli. Tacitus noted in his *Germania:*

> *They are always in the van and present a startling sight. Even in peace they decline to soften the savagery of their expression. None of them has home, land, or business of his own. To whatever host they choose to go, they get their keep from him, wasting the goods of others while despising their own.*

Not sharing a belief in Odin's talent for deception, Tacitus attributed the demise of these earliest Berserkers to "old age draining their blood and incapacitating" them.

BEAR MOTHER

In one culture or another, the bear has represented a range of prominent figures in human relationships—brother, father, cousin, grandfather or grandmother. However, in mythological terms the animal's most significant and ubiquitous role has been that of Bear Mother.

In the prototypical Bear Mother story, ursine divinities become alarmed at the blasphemy of human hunters and decide to intervene directly to put man right again. The ursine divinities do this by seducing or kidnapping a woman, then impregnating her. With this act, the sire dies for the good of the human tribe; the woman becomes a sacred progenitor and serves as the mediator between men and the bear world. It is through the woman that men recognize that they are part animal and part divinity and that their hunting activities are a sacred enterprise.

Directly connected to the Bear Mother myths are the Bear Son cycles, which follow the tortuous adventures of the son of a human mother and a bear god. As encapsulated in such epics as *Beowulf* and the *Odyssey*, the Bear Son endures a travail of attacks from monsters and betrayals by his companions as he seeks to establish his identity. Ultimately, the Bear Son concludes his journey and returns home to an adopted human father to marry a maiden who had given him up for lost. And although he is reconciled to his human nature, the Bear Son has also gained enough insight into his divine (bear) origins to be responsible to both worlds.

Northwind Picture Archives

HUNTING MYTHS

As central as combat has been to the Scandinavian and Teutonic appreciation of the bear, the proper way to hunt the animal has been equally significant among the other peoples of Northern Europe and Siberia. The Lapps, for example, reserve particular reverence for Leib-Olmai, a bear-god that not only protects the holy animal, but also provides the bear to hunters who have shown themselves worthy of it through prayer and sacrifice. In offering up their devotions to Leib-Olmai, the Lapps explicitly ask that the god not take the bear's side during the hunt.

Additionally, successful bear hunts precipitate more rituals as insurance against a dead bear's soul returning to avenge itself on the hunters: this is referred to as the apology mo-

tif. In the Ostyaks' exculpation ceremony, they cut off a dead animal's head, hang it on a tree, then gather in a circle to declare chorally (and politically):

> *Who killed you?*
> *It was the Russians.*
> *What cut off your head?*
> *It was a Russian ax.*
> *What will skin you?*
> *It will be a knife made by the Russians.*

For their part, the ancient Finns engaged in long rhetorical arguments with the dead bear in an attempt to persuade it that it was killed by a falling tree. More elaborately, the Lapps erected special huts to house the men involved in the kill. These men had to remain in the huts for three days so as not to contami-

THIS ILLUSTRATION DEPICTS
A NINETEENTH-CENTURY BEAR
HUNT.

THIS POLAR BEAR-SHAPED ESKIMO BOX WAS MADE IN SLEDGE ISLAND, ALASKA, AND WAS USED TO STORE THE BLADES THAT FIT ON THE ENDS OF WHALING-HARPOON HEADS. TO AID THEM IN THE HUNT, ESKIMOS OFTEN SUMMONED THE POWERS OF OTHER ANIMALS. THE POLAR BEAR, DUE TO ITS EFFECTIVE STALKING ABILITY, WAS OFTEN CALLED UPON TO AID IN SEAL AND WHALE HUNTS.

nate the rest of the tribe with their bloody deed. While in isolation, the hunters were also responsible for preparing the carcass for a festive meal. Only when the three days had ended and the meat had been shared by every member of the tribe were the hunters celebrated for their accomplishment.

The apology motif has always been significant among North American Indians as well. Among other tribes, the Malecites, Crees and Ottawas address a long list of their basic needs (food, clothing, warmth and so on) to the dead bear's carcass to justify having slain it. The Tlingits remind the bear that they would be poor without being able to hunt; the Western Carriers sing as they slay the animal so that it will be able to hear something pleasant as it dies. Other tribes have called for the hunter to put tobacco in the bear's mouth to assure it of the good intentions of the slayers.

Feasts organized to mark a successful hunt have also been riven between celebration and fear among many peoples. For instance, the Finns went so far as to call the feast a wedding and, to that end, dressed up a young man and a maiden as a bridegroom and bride for the occasion. At the same time, they sang songs to persuade the bear that it had died as a result of an accident not of their doing, that the house chosen for the feast was worthy of its victim, and that all the cooking preparations were in accordance with its sacred nature. Toward the end of the meal, the Finns sounded another reverential note; all the guests asked the dead bear to persuade its fellow creatures to make themselves available for future hunts for the tribe's survival.

A particular concern of the Ostyaks, and of many North American tribes, was that the slaughtered bear ask other bears not to attack the village livestock. To get the animal's agreement, a woman celebrant set a plate of food before the carcass and intoned:

Do not touch the horses
do not touch the cows
now that I have placed
the dish before thee.

Other Ostyak incantations asked that the bear neither attack women who were gathering berries nor children who had wandered away from the village.

Aside from hunting associations, the bear entered the lives of Finno-Ugric peoples in a variety of other ways that attested to its divine status. Similar to the ways that Christian cultures have put stock in swearing on the Bible, the Ostyaks and the Voguls took their oaths in the name of the bear. Another one of their customs was the way in which suspected delinquents defended themselves; they were to bite the hair of a bear carcass and declare: "If I am in the wrong, then bite me just as I have bitten you."

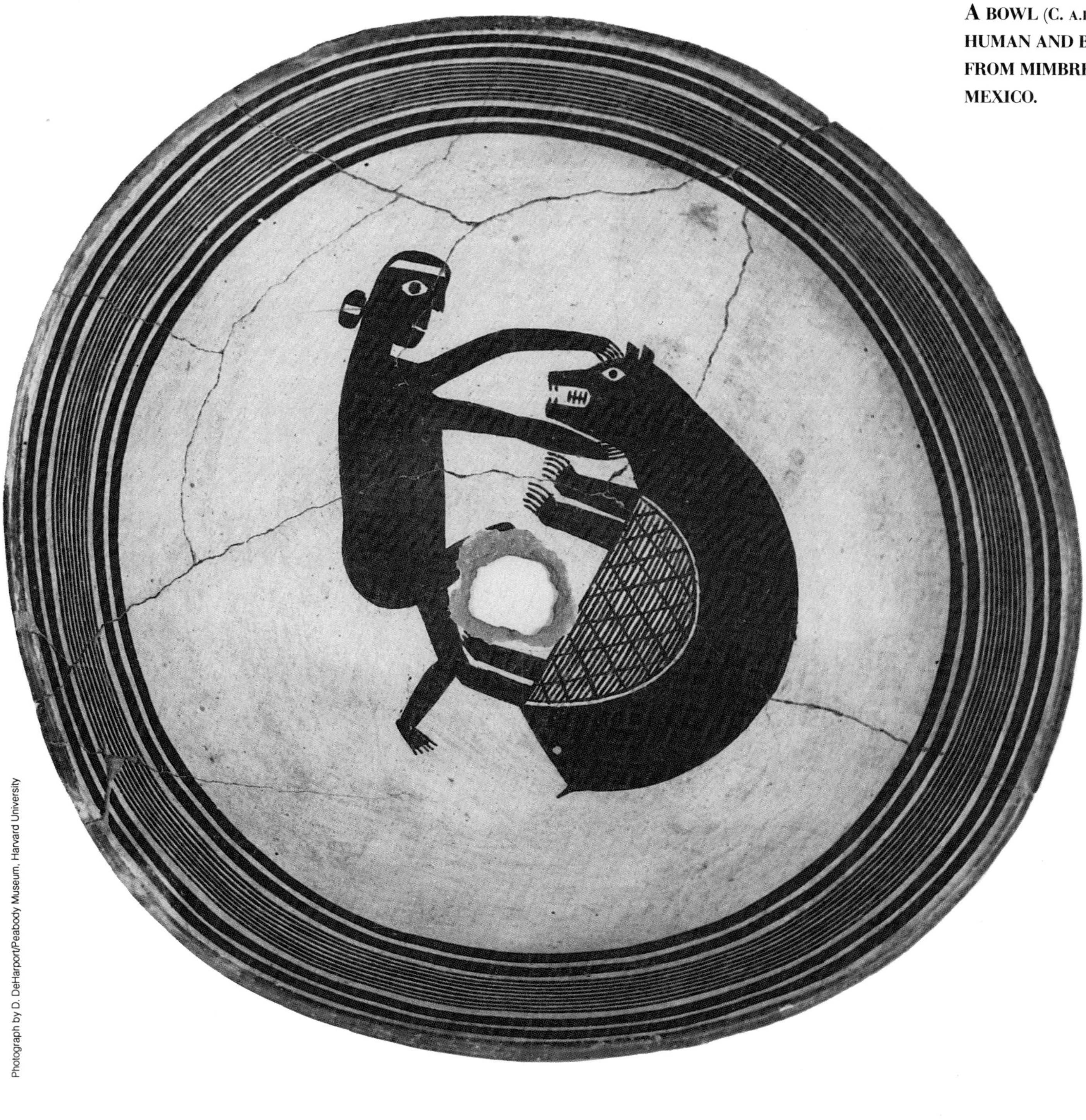

A BOWL (C. A.D. 750–1150) WITH HUMAN AND BEAR DESIGN FROM MIMBRES VALLEY, NEW MEXICO.

Photograph by D. DeHarport/Peabody Museum, Harvard University

CHAPTER

4

BROWN
BEARS

The brown bear *(Ursus arctos)* often defies expectation. First, its coloring is just as likely to be blue-black, red, cinnamon, tan or chocolate as it is brown. Second, despite the enormous size of some of its subspecies, the brown bear is something less than the most stout-hearted of hunters when it is in the mood for meat; it generally prefers young, disabled or abandoned game to healthy, adult deer or caribou. And while this bear has certainly amassed a significant number of rash human victims over the ages, it clearly tends to favor threatening growls and flight over homicide where intrusive humans are concerned.

DISTRIBUTION

From the arctic seas crowning Asia, Europe and North America, and as far south as Iran, Spain and Mexico, brown bears claim most of the northern hemisphere as home. Subspecies, some of which weigh a ton or more, include the Siberian brown bear *(Ursus arctos beringianus)*, the Himalayan red bear *(Ursus arctos isabellinus)*, the Manchurian brown bear *(Ursus arctos manchuricus)*, the horse bear of Tibet and western China *(Ursus arctos horribilis)* and the Alaskan Kodiak bear *(Ursus arctos middendorffi)*. These bears range so widely in appearance and habitat that until the beginning of this century, many naturalists treated them as separate species; only in recent decades have these bears been grouped together as a single family with a dozen or so subspecies.

For all its ubiquitousness, the brown bear has been waging an ominous battle against

extinction. In the last three hundred years, it has completely disappeared from such traditional haunts as Germany, Switzerland and Holland. Today it can be found in Western Europe only in scattered areas of Spain, Italy and Norway. Of the eighteen thousand brown bears estimated as surviving in Europe, almost all of them are concentrated between Yugoslavia and the Western European regions of the Soviet Union.

ALTHOUGH THE KODIAK, TOP, HAS SEEN ITS RANGING AREAS RELENTLESSLY REDUCED IN RECENT YEARS, THE PROBLEM IS SOMEWHAT MORE SEVERE FOR ITS COUSIN, THE EUROPEAN BROWN BEAR, BOTTOM.

In other parts of the world, brown bears have not fared much better. In step with its disappearance from Western Europe, the brown bear has vanished completely from North Africa over the last couple of centuries. Within the continental United States, only several hundred bears now inhabit a handful of northwestern states. In Japan, the government has become so alarmed by the decline of brown bears that it has forbidden the Ainu people to continue their ancient tradition of killing and eating a captured cub during a winter festival organized to placate the bear-gods. In fact, aside from the Asian and Siberian zones of the Soviet Union (brown bear population of one hundred thousand) and Canada and Alaska (twenty thousand), the brown bear has suffered a diminution over the last three hundred years at a rate comparable to some of the worst cases of animal extinction.

For the most part, the brown bear's decimation has been attributed to the steady expansion of human settlements into its traditional ranging areas, but two other factors also seem to have played a part in its decline. First, the unusually ferocious appearance of such subspecies as the grizzly, according to some experts on the question, has caused much more gratuitous killing (through poisoned traps, for instance) of brown bears than of other species.

Second, although no bear species has profited from the nearness of cities, highways or the bulldozers used to lay their foundations, brown bears in particular have shown little tolerance for the proximity of human beings; this leads them to retreat into increasingly smaller grazing districts, where their food problems have grown even more precarious.

Also affected has been the brown bears' traditional foraging at any time during the night or day. European browns, for instance, are now active mainly in the late afternoon and early evening. Even open-country bears, like Alaska's Kodiaks and grizzlies, have become much warier of their increasingly human-filled sur-

roundings and no longer wander around as freely in daylight as their ancestors did.

The established shyness of the brown bear has reduced the portrayals of the Kodiaks and grizzlies, in particular, to aggressive man-eaters forever on the prowl for human prey. If any member of the *Ursus arctos* family still needs a better image, it is probably the horse bear, which has been charged with killing up to 1,500 farmers a year in the mountains flanking the Tibetan Plateau. Lacking more precise information, Western naturalists have noted that the region has been the subject of an intensive cultivation program and have speculated that Chinese and Tibetan farmers, undoubtedly armed only with shovels and hoes, have sought to drive the bears away from desirable land and succeeded only in enraging the animal. In any case, not too much credence has been given to the figure of 1,500 annual fatalities.

PHYSICAL TRAITS

In appearance, the brown bear is particularly stout and chunky, with a big hump of fat and muscle over its shoulders. It has long claws on its forefeet that enable it to dig easily for ground squirrels or other burrowing game; unless seriously worn down from use, the claws extend more than 2 in. The massive, wide head of the brown bear has prompted many observers to describe it as "dish-faced" and has also served as the inspiration for the commercial teddy bear. Its extraordinarily powerful jaws have been known to chomp completely through pine-tree trunks of more than 8 in. in diameter.

The size of brown bears varies widely. The largest member of the family is presumed to

be the Alaskan Kodiak, which can reach 1,800 lbs., with the Siberian brown bear not too far behind. Continental American grizzlies sometimes grow as large as 1,500 lbs., while their significantly smaller cousins in Alaska rarely top more than half that. At the lightest end of the scale is the Syrian brown bear of the northeast Mediterranean, normally little

© John T. Turner/FPG International

AN ALASKAN GRIZZLY
ROAMING ITS RANGE.

more than 400 lbs. Other brown bears' weight is between that of the Siberians and the Syrians.

For some years now, researchers have been intrigued by reports of a subspecies even larger than the Kodiak on the Kamchatka Peninsula in the southeast extremity of the Soviet Union. Because of the peninsula's numerous military bases and severely restricted public access, however, knowledge of the monster-bear has remained mostly hearsay. Lacking concrete evidence to the contrary, researchers believe that the animals in question are probably just particularly large Siberian brown bears.

HUNTING AND EATING HABITS

Although their winter denning serves as the chief reference point for their eating habits, brown bears vary their diets according to the seasons. Animal meat accounts for about 20 percent of their annual intake, with the rest divided among plants, fish, eggs and insects. A typical mapping of the brown bear's quest for food from the moment that it emerges from its winter resting place progresses something like this: first, the bear meanders down into valleys or toward coastal areas in search of new plant shoots. After a couple of weeks of this light fare, it then ambles up the hillsides in search of ants, bird eggs and the earliest berries. Usually coinciding with the onset of summer, the bear then migrates toward the rivers or seas for spawning salmon and other fish. Kodiaks and Siberian browns fish for almost a month, while other browns ply inland waters for slightly less time. In both instances, the bear shows a marked preference for eating the eggs of the female fish to eating a whole male and usually discards the remnants of the mother for other bears or scavengers. The dominant male bear customarily does its fishing at a spot just below a waterfall, while other bears scatter themselves further down along shallow shores.

When the bear has had its fill of fish and roe, it heads back up the surrounding hills or mountains, climbing even further than on its earlier expedition, looking for mushrooms, nuts and more mature berries. At this point, it will show more of an appetite for meat and zero in on small deer and elk or caribou calves, especially if the latter have been wounded or orphaned by hunters. When a bear kills more game than it can eat, it will bury the animal and stand guard over it for a future meal. Finally, at the end of summer and early autumn, the animal will generally hunt in mountain clearings and depend on its long claws for digging up squirrels, marmots, mice and other subterranean prey.

Of course, each subspecies of the brown bear has its own hunting and foraging peculiarities, dictated for the most part by the terrain. Unlike the average bear, whose diet is 20 percent meat, Japanese brown bears rely on vegetation for almost their entire food consumption, the principal exceptions being flying insects and an occasional sample of livestock. To avoid attacks on their animals, farmers in various regions of Asia have sought to develop grain-eating habits among bears by setting aside patches of land and growing oats specifically for them. In Czechoslovakia

BEARS LEARN HOW TO FISH AT A YOUNG AGE.

BY MIDSUMMER, MOST BIG BROWN BEARS LIKE THE ALASKAN GRIZZLY ARE CONSUMING 90 POUNDS OF FOOD A DAY.

and other parts of Eastern Europe, brown bears have shown a special fondness for the sap of spruce and fir trees.

One of the more detailed observations of the eating habits of the Alaskan grizzly was made some years ago by naturalist Adolph Murie. From May, when the animal emerged from denning, to the end of September, Murie noted that the animal had consumed 721 different meal substances; various grasses (277 types) and roots (239) were the most frequently digested fare, while horsetail grass (104) was the single-most-eaten item. On the other hand, Murie listed only twenty-nine pieces of carrion, the majority of which were caribou and moose calves.

Despite Murie's observations and the idiosyncracies of the plant eaters of Japan, however, brown bears generally remain second only to polar bears in their taste for meat. Although late-summer kills of abandoned or ailing ungulates provide meat, bears get most of it from the carcasses of dead deer and other animals that have been preserved in ice over the winter. The bears dig up the remains, along with berries and roots, shortly after they emerge from their winter dens.

HIBERNATION AND REPRODUCTION

By high summer, the largest brown bears are taking in as much as 90 lbs. of food a day, which amounts to a daily gain of about 5 lbs. of fat. As northern-hemisphere creatures facing relatively long winters, brown bears have been known to exceed this daily intake so they can reach an average protective fat layer of 6 in. prior to denning.

Brown bears begin laying the foundations for their dens around the third or fourth week of September. The ideal location is generally dry earth on a slope underneath a big boulder or the roots of a sizable tree. Interior dimensions will vary according to each subspecies. Some Russian bears have been found to build dwellings as tight as 5 ft. long, 3.5 ft. wide and about 2.5 ft. high. More typical dimensions for the brown bear den are 7 ft. long, 7 ft. wide and 3 ft. high, but some lairs are even larger to accommodate pregnant females or mothers and their cubs. Many of the dens have short tunnels that separate the outside from the sleeping chamber proper. Except in rainy areas, where ground collapses are common, a den can endure for generations and be used by different bears in successive winters. In some zones where denning possibilities are limited, as many as a dozen bears will dig in under boulders, trees or even logs within a square mile or so of one another.

The principal exceptions to the practice of winter denning among brown bears are males that have not fattened up enough to retire for the winter. Still in need of nutrition, they usually find a haystack or some other point of relative concealment so that they can continue to search for the scant food possibilities that exist in the snow. These animals are regarded as particularly dangerous to men, but their lack of an adequate fat layer can ultimately prove more fatal to the bears themselves.

Most brown bears will enter their dens with the first snows, so as to leave no tracks behind them. Inside, they will have prepared a bed of pine needles, leaves and grasses anywhere from 8 to 12 in. thick. As a further precaution against intruders, many brown bears will rake some of the vegetation into the den entrance. If not giving birth or nursing cubs, they are able to sleep in the same position for as long as a month, without urinating or defecating.

Depending on the weather, some brown bears will stick their muzzles out of the den as early as February to warm themselves in the sun, but generally will remain inside for another couple of months. February also is generally when brown bears give birth. The average litter is two cubs; infant grizzlies weigh about 5 lbs., and new Siberian browns can weigh as much as 14 lbs. Like other cubs, brown bear cubs will not open their eyes for at least four weeks.

When the bears emerge from their dens around the beginning of April, they show clear signs of weakness and grogginess from their hibernation and for a couple of days are up to little more than eating snow and the most accessible roots. Their first dietary order of business is purging themselves of the hardened plant material that has blocked the rectum during the winter, and to this end they will consume large amounts of tender shoots. It is only after a week or two of this intake that they will begin to reverse their winter weight loss. During the denning, brown bears will have burned up about 4,000 calories a day and lost about 30 percent of their fat layer; it will take several weeks for them to return to their predenning weight.

Cubs are especially vulnerable to attacks by adult males in the first weeks of spring, when the mother bears are still weak from denning, although this danger persists until the offspring have survived another winter and reach an age of eighteen or twenty months. Estimates are that as much as 40 percent of brown bear cubs are killed before reaching their second birthday. When the cubs reach their third year, their mothers usually abandon them, then prepare for another mating that will reinstigate the cycle.

CUBS HAVE TO BE ESPECIALLY WARY OF ATTACKS FROM ADULT MALES IN THE FIRST WEEKS OF SPRING BECAUSE THEIR MOTHER IS STILL WEAK FROM HER PROLONGED DENNING.

CHAPTER

5

THE BEAR IN
LEGEND AND
LITERATURE

In view of the bear's entrenched position in so many pre-Christian cultures and mythologies, it is hardly surprising that the creature became a frequent target for the animus of the Church scholars who produced most early Western writings. When the bear wasn't being excoriated as a symbol for the devil, it was usually presented as an allegorical object lesson in base behavior. In fact, through the agency of one Church father or another, the bear eventually managed the conspicuous feat of representing every one of Christian theology's seven capital sins.

One of the earliest texts to warn against the bear and its attributes was the *Physiologus*, a collection of second- and third-century sermons that was cited as an authoritative preachment by theologians for almost a thousand years. In one form or another, the sermons were recited from Iceland to Asia Minor, used as a basis for school instruction, quoted by popes and illustrated in monasteries and churches. The *Physiologus* (and subsequent translators and adaptors) said the bear is:

> *... a beast clumsy by nature and unable to run easily like the other beasts, but rather drags itself along slowly. It prefers to bury itself in the ground and to keep itself hidden in a hole, for its limbs are not adapted to convey swiftly such a monstrous body. In the time of cold it always stays in a hole.*

> *The Bear is like unto us, because he presents an image and picture of sin, which is clumsy and hangs on man and drags after him so that he is held backward. And he runs not easily; that is, the Devil does not urge him suddenly into sin; but he moves slowly, that is, the hunter by artifice beguiles him into a desire for sin. And he loves to hide and bury himself in his lurking place, that is, in that which satisfies his desires. Also in the time of cold he is wont to keep himself tightly in his hole, that is, when man is snared through his lust the Devil brings him into the pit prepared for him and holds him for his entire life. . . .*

If the *Physiologus* treated the bear as a symbolic admonishment against sin in general, other early European writings were more specific in their indictment. In an untitled eighth-century Latin poem attributed to Paulus Diaconus, for instance, the bear was viewed as the epitome of a justly punished calumny. The poem, a medieval adaptation

of an Aesopic fable, tells of a lion that falls ill and summons other animals in the hope of finding a cure for his malady. All answer the lion's call except the fox, whose absence is exploited by a bear that suggests that the missing animal is, at the very least, indifferent to the lion's fate. The lion reacts by condemning the fox to death, but the fox soon arrives on the scene to explain that he has been on a long journey in search of a remedy for the lion's ailment. The cure? The lion should be wrapped in a bear's skin. In the end, the supposedly ill-meaning bear is flayed alive, the lion cured and the fox rewarded.

GREED AND GLUTTONY

Greed and gluttony characterize the bear in the Reynard Cycle, the most influential of all medieval beast sagas. Published in the thirteenth century as the apparent outcome of fused Flemish, German and French oral traditions, one of the cycle's most noted tales concerns a bear named Bruin and his hapless attempts to carry out an order to bring Reynard the fox to court to answer for his crimes. Knowing the bear's weakness for honey, Reynard distracts Bruin from his mission and leads him to a great oak tree, the trunk of

EXTREME GLUTTONY WAS JUST ONE OF THE MANY NEGATIVE TRAITS ATTRIBUTED TO THE BEAR.

THESE DRAWINGS WERE TAKEN FROM THE REYNARD CYCLE, THE MOST INFLUENTIAL OF THE MEDIEVAL BEAST SAGAS.

which is split with the cleft held open by wedges. As soon as the bear reaches inside for the honeycombs, he is trapped by the wedges. This is only the beginning of Bruin's troubles because his cries of pain bring the carpenter Lantfert to the scene:

> *And Lantfert came and found the Bear fast taken in the tree. Then he ran fast to his neighbors and said: "Come all into my yard— there is a bear taken!" The word anon sprang over all in the thorp. There ne remained neither man ne wife, but all ran thither as fast as they could, every one with his weapon—some with a staff, some with a rake, some with a broom, some with a stake of the hedge and some with a flail. And the priest of the Church had the staff of the Cross and the clerk carried a vane. The priest's wife Julocke came with her distaff—she*

sat then and span. There came old women that for age had not one tooth in their head. Now was Bruin the Bear nigh much care that he alone had to stand against them all. When he heard all this great noise and cry, he wrestled and plucked so hard and so sore that he got out of his head. But he left behind all the skin and both his ears, in such wise that never man saw fouler ne loathier beast, for the blood ran over his eyes. And ere he could get out his feet he must leave there his claws or nails and his rough hand. This traffic comes to him evil, for he supposed never to have gone, his feet were so sore, and he did not see for the blood that ran over his eyes. . . .

Although he barely survives his self-inflicted wounds and those subsequently administered by Lantfert and his neighbors, Bruin, as one widespread reading of the tale had it, has learned something about the perils of "gluttony and pursuing the sweet things of life."

In obvious debt to the Reynard Cycle, or to the tradition informing it, a later Norwegian folk story promotes an identical lesson, except that wasps instead of villagers act as the agents of the bear's punishment. More directly, the fourteenth-century Wycliffite Bible declared that men were called bears because of greed and gluttony and would be so punished. The medieval French homilist Odo of Cluny warned that the "voracity of bears" was an evil that required severe correction in convents, and early manuscripts of Chaucer's *Canterbury Tales* illustrated "The Parson's Tale" by showing Gluttony riding a bear.

LUST

Even more prevalent than the bear as a symbol of gluttony was its use for dramatizing the sinfulness of lust and fornication. (The fourteenth-century Swedish mystic St. Bridget gave the bear *both* gluttony and lechery as principal attributes.) In a typical poem by the thirteenth-century German mystic Mechthild of Magdeburg, the soul was described as being in battle with four sins represented by animals; the bear played the role of unsanctioned sex. In several Gothic tales about vice and virtue that were published in the fourteenth and fifteenth centuries, texts and accompanying graphics repeatedly depicted Luxuria and Lascivia riding bears or having some other ursine identification. The sixteenth-century Virgil Solis employed the bear in ornamental engravings as a partner for the ape in symbolizing impure love—both of these animals were usually contrasted with the chaste unicorn. Also numerous were scholastic texts that warned that the punishment for a dissolute life was to wear a bear's skull in hell for eternity.

A common motif of medieval European fables and folktales was for a sexually despotic bear to exact a maiden as the price for either helping or desisting from attacking her father. In one Russian version of the tale, the bear takes the eldest sister and has his way with her until she disobeys him by sticking her hand in his tar deposits. Although her thumb falls off upon contact with the tar, the bear does not see this as sufficient punishment and kills her. This routine is repeated with a second sister and is about to recur with a third, pure sister, when the guilt-ridden father rescues her from the bear. To drive home the point of the tale, the fleeing girl calls the animal a bandy-legged Satan in a context that makes it clear that the sexual attentions of the bear to the sisters were worse sins than the two murders.

In a typical Armenian tale, a maiden is not very happy about being forced to live with a bear but tries to make the best of it for a while. When an opportunity at last presents itself for her escape, she seizes it, only to be condemned to a disfigurement of her face for having tarried too long in the bear's bed.

"Juan Oso," a Mexican tale of European origin that echoes some of the oldest bear creation myths, tells of the faithless Maria, who abandons her husband to live with a bear, then becomes entrapped between her passion for and fear of the animal. She gives birth to the title character, who is half-man, half-bear; he eventually leads her back to her original husband. Of course, penance and redemption await her.

In some cases, the association of the bear with unbridled lust was combined with an anthropomorphic motif to contrast pure and impure love, as well as to stress that procre-

ation was the purpose of copulation. An exemplary tale of this kind is the Norwegian "White Bear King Valemon":

The king's daughter has her heart set on a golden wreath. The king has many made for her, but she rejects them all as imperfect. One day in the forest, she sees the wreath she has been looking for in the paws of a white bear. The animal agrees to give the princess the wreath, but only on condition that she will receive him at her father's castle in three days, then leave with him in marriage. Despite the king's attempts to fob off his two uglier daughters as replacements, the bear exacts his price and returns to the forest with the princess.

There, the bear establishes a routine of seeing his beloved only at night in their dark bedroom; otherwise he stays away from the cabin. This routine is maintained for three years, during which the princess gives birth to three children, whom the bear immediately takes away to a secret place. Finally, and in spite of the bear's warnings never to cast a light on him at night, the princess smuggles a candle into the bedroom and discovers that the bear is actually a man. In anguish, the man explains that if the princess had only obeyed him for another day, he would have been free of a witch's spell that had turned him into a bear and that he could have returned to a human state permanently; thanks to her unfortunate disobedience, he now has to fulfill a vow to marry the witch.

The following morning, the princess sees her beloved scampering away from the house, once again in the form of a bear. She chases but cannot catch him. Exhausted, she stops off at a farmhouse where a child points out the bear's trail and gives her a present. The princess has similar encounters in two other

THIS PAINTING, "IVAN," BY CARL C.M. RUNGIUS, CONVEYS A DIGNIFIED IMAGE OF THE BEAR, UNLIKE THE MANY MYTHS AND LEGENDS THAT ATTRIBUTE NEGATIVE QUALITIES TO THE ANIMAL.

farmhouses with two other children. Finally, the princess arrives at the castle of the witch; with the help of the gifts from the children, she outmaneuvers the hag and breaks the spell on her beloved. Her husband then explains that the children who helped her find him were actually their own and that he had known all along that the children were the only way they could forge a stronger bond than sexual union. The princess and her husband retrieve the children and live happily ever after.

The Church ideal of matrimony was not the only sacramental defense against the bear's lustful ways. For instance, there is the North German story of the Teutonic knight who, resting in a forest, is approached by a she-bear and propositioned. When he declines her favors, he is immediately reduced to a state of dementia. At the second invitation from the bear, he agrees to have sex with her, but only on condition that she is first baptized. The bear accepts the stipulation, receives the sacrament and is transformed into a beautiful maiden who marries her savior.

Even relatively "enlightened" views of women who have lost their virginity maintain a strong metaphorical link with the bear or with its habits. Thus, the seventeenth-century Bishop of Genoa, St. Francis de Sales, observed in his tract *The Devout Life* that "undamaged fruit can be preserved in straw, sand, or its own leaves; but once bruised it

can be preserved only in sugar or honey; similarly there are many ways of preserving chastity when it is unimpaired, but once violated it can only be preserved by the sugar and honey of a very strong devotion."

SLOTH

After gluttony and lust, the bear in medieval Europe also had to answer to charges of sloth. The *Ancrene Riwle*, a twelfth-century book of conduct for the nuns of England, warned its readers against falling into the "heavy sloth" common to bears. Another compilation of behavioral vices and virtues, *Secreta Secretorum*, scolded man for being like a "wayk and sleuthfull" bear. In the fifteenth century, the bear was often pictured in the company of the idle grasshopper and was an object of such rhymed lessons as:

> *Who'll never glean in Summer's heat*
> *In Winter will have naught to eat.*

Many of the folktales pitting the bear against the nimble fox, such as in the Reynard Cycle, stress that it is the bear's essential laziness together with its gluttony that makes it vulnerable to deception. Various Baltic fables repeat this theme by claiming that the bear lost its tail by taking the fox's suggestion that it was a more effective fishing instrument than its paws.

The bear was also used as a symbol of anger and violence. To this end, many medieval scribes and storytellers dusted off various Old Testament descriptions of the animal as being an agent of God's wrath. Among these was Jeremiah's observation in *Lamentations* that God in His anger was like a bear lying in wait. There also was the *Book of Hosea*'s testimony of divine pique: "I am the Lord your

God. . . . they forgot me. So I will be to them like a lion, I will fall upon them like a bear robbed of her cubs."

Cited even more frequently was the incident in 2 *Kings* 2:24, in which God calls upon two she-bears to tear apart the forty-two children of Bethel for mocking the aged prophet Elisha. Although the original instruction of the episode had been aimed at underscoring the importance of showing reverence for the elderly, the medieval moralists equally stressed that only a bear had the necessary ferocity to serve as an instrument of God's ire. As Bartholomeus Anglicus, the thirteenth-century English encyclopedist, said: "No beest hath so grete sleyghte to do evyll dedes as the bear."

The same emphasis of ferocity appeared in the twelfth-century *Hortus Deliciarum*, where the bear was depicted as signifying brute force, and in popular stories of the period in which various saints were tormented to martyrdom by the animal. A Basque story of the era tells of a blacksmith who hammered hot iron so violently on his anvil that the sparks reached the eye of God. To punish the impudent smith for having singed him, God turned him into a bear "in accordance with nature." A number of Renaissance engravings throughout Europe carried on this association; one especially familiar motif showed an ugly or deformed human being who symbolized wrath in the company of a bear.

REGENERATION

The bear's positive connotations for medieval Church moralists were mainly in connection with the belief that cubs were born amorphous and were literally licked into shape by their mothers. For Christian writers, this new, more sophisticated perception of the bear

provided an antidote to the animal's negative grip on popular imagination since it suggested that the Church could combat paganism and animism with the transformable and regenerative power of its sacraments. It was in this spirit that so many of the earliest saints of the Church (a partial list would include Gall, Blandina, Columba, Korbinian, Sergius and Maximus) were portrayed as having tamed the animal, frequently to the point of making it a mascot. According to Shepard and Sanders's *Sacred Paw*, Korbinian was once on his way to Rome when he and his pack animals were attacked by a bear. Not only did the saint remain undaunted by the bear, but he used the strength of his faith to force the animal to replace the slain pack horses and carry the baggage for the rest of the trip.

While the Church's "optimism" emerged occasionally in the written word and graphic arts of the Middle Ages, it flourished during the Renaissance. A typical bear tale of this period was *The Masquerade of Orson and*

THE BELIEF THAT MOTHER BEARS LICKED THEIR CUBS INTO SHAPE PROVIDED A METAPHOR FOR CHURCH MORALISTS, WHO BELIEVED THAT THE CHURCH COULD COMBAT PAGANISM AND ANIMISM WITH THE REGENERATIVE POWER OF ITS SACRAMENTS.

Valentine, a sixteenth-century English translation of an earlier French romance. In this tale, twin infants are abandoned in a forest. One eventually makes his way to the court of King Pippin, where he is given the name Valentine; the other is raised as an animal by bears and is known as the Nameless. Years later, Valentine encounters his twin, tames him so that he turns into a loyal servant of the court and has him baptized Orson so that he remembers his feral beginnings and will remain grateful for his salvation.

A series of engravings by the sixteenth-century French artist Theodore de Brie showed a she-bear licking its whelp accompanied by the specific instruction that natural forces could be shaped—and even be made beautiful—through patient education. Other painters of the period joined the figure of Cupid to the licking bear to impart the lesson that time gradually perfects uncultivated love. No less a Renaissance figure than Titian adopted a she-bear as his personal insignia with the motto *Natura potentior ars* ("art is more powerful than nature").

In *Henry VI*, Shakespeare equated chaos with "an unlicked bear whelp" for describing the stage of preorder. A little later, in his *Dun-*

ciad, the poet Alexander Pope embraced approvingly the image of a bear mother:

> *So watchful Bruin forms,*
> *with plastic care*
> *Each growing lump,*
> *and brings it to a bear.*

In retrospect at least, this single behavioral characteristic of the bear mother seems to have almost counterbalanced the welter of other attributes assigned to the animal over the ages. Even more ironically, the sacramental powers of Christianity have become a figurative reflection of a mother bear licking its litter into shape. On this premise, of course, the bear's other qualities—in particular, its strength—are also seen as ultimately working for, rather than against, Christianity. In fact, one might say that, in many respects, Christianity has adopted the bear almost as credulously as ancient mythologies did.

THE BEAR AS ANTI-INTELLECTUAL SYMBOL

But even with the Church's more complex views of the bear, it was not out·of the woods where censorious imaginations were concerned. On the contrary, the same qualities that made the bear metaphorically controllable to Renaissance artists and theologians— its tameability and fidelity, for instance—were what made it less acceptable to more analytic minds. Not to put too fine a point on it, the bear, whether being presented as a negative or positive object lesson, whether being deceived by the fox or taking on the burden of a saint, frequently came off as simply stupid. While some scholars have bent over backwards to reinterpret the Reynard Cycle and

other popular tales to argue that the bear had more guile than its enemies, there has remained a significant body of imagery identifying the animal with an aversion to cerebral functions.

For the eighteenth-century Swedish philosopher Emanuel Swedenborg, the bear and its attributes added up to the very opposite of clear thinking: "Bears signify fallacies—the literal sense of the Word, read indeed, but not understood." In this century, the Austrian novelist Robert Musil was even more explicit when a character in *The Man Without Qualities* tells another: "It's really history that has always had the bearish or the bullish tendencies where speculation in mankind is concerned—in the bearish manner, by means of cunning and violence; in the bullish more or less the way your life is trying to do it here, by means of believing in the power of ideas. . . ."

The American poet Robert Frost added another wrinkle to the bear's mental limita-

tions when he suggested in his 1928 poem "The Bear" that the animal was similar to man insofar as yes, indeed, it *could* think— but purely destructively, to the arrogant point that it believed it could resolve anything by ruminating long enough. Frost wrote:

> *He sits back on his fundamental butt*
> *With lifted snout and eyes (if any) shut*
> *(He almost looks religious but he's not),*
> *And back and forth he sways from cheek*
> *   to cheek,*
> *At one extreme agreeing with one Greek,*
> *At the other agreeing with another Greek,*
> *Which may be thought, but only so to*
> *   speak.*
> *A baggy figure, equally pathetic*
> *When sedentary and when peripatetic.*

In sum, short of the perception of the animal as the symbol of the hothouse effect, humans have been hard put to find any emotional, physical, mental or moral endeavor that cannot be represented by the bear.

CHAPTER

6

POLAR
BEARS

As he scanned the waters of the polar ice cap, Lincoln Ellsworth felt very good about himself. He had reason to: the year was 1926, and the naturalist-explorer was a member of the first transpolar flight. But then, 4 degrees south of the North Pole, Ellsworth's self-congratulation receded before the sight of a lone track across an ice floe. "What a mockery to our egotism," he declared later concerning his first encounter with a polar bear. "Yet, there it was, plainly crossing the floe, something alive and, like ourselves, seeking. . . ."

PHYSICAL TRAITS

To the polar bear, the five million miles of circumpolar coast, sea and islands are·a life-sustaining realm and have been since the mid-Pleistocene epoch (between one hundred thousand and two hundred thousand years ago), when the polar bear was thought to have evolved from the Siberian brown bear during its glacial advances north. Forced by their new environment to hunt seals and other arctic mammals for their survival, polar bears gradually became more carnivorous than their ancestors; they also developed sharper teeth for shearing flesh and more refined claws that were better suited to grasping squirming prey than to ferreting out roots. The most radical change was in their color: creamy white in winter and yellowish white in summer, polar bears cannot be mistaken for any of their relatives. Like the snow and ice of its habitat, the polar bear's coat is unpigmented; it derives its whiteness from internal reflections from the snow and ice in the nearly hollow shafts of its hairs. By capturing the sun's ultraviolet energy, this also serves to keep the animal warm.

The largest of the polar bears, "the great lonely roamers," as they are called by the Eskimos, average 9 ft. in length. While females stop growing at four years and weigh slightly less than 700 lbs., males continue to develop until they are twice as old and weigh twice as much; the largest polar bear on record measured well over 12 ft. and an incredible 2,210 lbs. In general, only Kodiaks surpass polar bears in size among the world's terrestrial carnivores.

GREAT TRAVELERS, POLAR BEARS WILL COVER SOME 104,000 SQUARE MILES IN THEIR LIFETIMES.

Color and size are not the polar bear's only distinctions. It has a longer neck and smaller head than other bears do and is the only bear with fur padding the soles of its feet, which provides better traction on ice. Its enormous forepaws (up to 12 in. in diameter) have webbed membranes that allow it to swim and tread water more efficiently; in fact, in the water, the polar bear paddles only with the forepaws and trails its hind legs behind. These bears have better use for their rear limbs on land, where they can run as fast as 25 mi. an hour in pursuit of prey. But for the most part, they attain such speeds only for short bursts, since the same metabolism that is so well geared for conserving heat in a cold environment is ill-suited for cooling off.

As their migratory routes suggest, polar bears are also great travelers. They cover about 100,000 sq. mi. in a lifetime, for the most part in a steady, ponderous shuffle of about 2.5 mi. an hour. Because of their massive legs and general build, they expend far more energy walking than do other carnivores of comparable size and require frequent rest stops. When moving down an embankment or steep hillside, they are likely to get into a semireclining position and use their front legs as brakes.

Polar bears are gifted with exceptional eyesight and hearing, easily equal to man's. Their sense of smell is so extraordinary that they are able to detect a seal or whale carcass from as far away as 20 mi. Like some of their southern cousins, polar bears have also shown an ability to foil human snares set for them; for instance, several witnesses have reported cases of the animals triggering traps with huge rocks so they could get the bait without putting themselves at risk.

© Mark Newman/Tom Stack & Associates

FUR PADS THE SOLES OF THE POLAR BEAR'S FEET TO PROVIDE BETTER TRACTION ON ICE.

DISTRIBUTION

Polar bears (*Ursus maritimus*) are indigenous to the arctic and subarctic regions of five countries—the United States, Canada, the Soviet Union, Norway and the Danish territory of Greenland. Polar bears remain mainly on the coasts and southern broken edges of the polar ice pack and rarely venture far out into the open sea or more than a few miles inland. Notable exceptions in recent decades include one male that was spotted at 88 degrees latitude, only 2 degrees away from the North Pole itself, and a female that was shot several miles inland in Quebec.

Once believed to be in constant circular migration around the pole, polar bears are now known to have distinct area populations; each population has its own migratory pattern. The bears of Greenland and Northern Canada, for example, drift southward on the floating ice pack from Baffin Island down to Hudson Bay and James Bay during spring and late summer; by August, when the ice has disintegrated, they start heading back north along the coastline, eventually returning to their denning grounds above the arctic circle. In the arctic seas above Scandinavia, the bears have a lateral migration, west to east, as they summer on the Norwegian islands of Spitsbergen and Northeastland, and den up several hundred miles to the east in Franz Josef Land, a cluster of islands in Soviet territory. Alaskan polar bears migrate through the Bering Strait to the Chukchi Sea.

LIFE ON THE BROKEN EDGES OF THE POLAR ICE PACK.

HUNTING AND EATING HABITS

The polar bear's preferred diet includes ringed and bearded seals and walrus calves; it will also make a meal of shoreline carrion like beached whales, fish and shellfish. Much of the bear's hunting regimen is a prowl on the ice for mother seals and pups in the *nunarjaks* (snow-covered birth lairs). A seal coming up for air at a blow-hole is also a common target; a single smack from the bear's paw will crush its skull. A seal napping on the ice near water is more difficult for the polar bear to snare; and in these more challenging instances, the bear must use all its agility and guile (including covering up its black snout), dodge behind snowbanks and ice ridges, get down in a cat-

© Wolfgang Kaehler

like creep and suddenly rise and rush to claim its victim before it can slip away.

After killing a seal, a bear will suck out its fat, often leaving an entire skin turned deftly inside out—blubberless, but otherwise intact. Many scientists believe that the fat is even more important to the bear's diet than meat is, because meat requires large quantities of fresh water for aiding digestion, and that water is simply not present during an arctic winter. In fact, the polar bear's thirst is legendary among the Eskimos. When a Baffin Island hunter has killed one of the animals, he pays it a final tribute by melting some ice in his own mouth and then dripping the water into the bear's jaw.

In late summer, after the melting of the ice pack has made hunting seals impossible, polar bears resort to blueberries, mushrooms, grasses, duck eggs and lemmings for survival.

ONLY KODIAKS SURPASS POLAR BEARS IN SIZE AMONG THE WORLD'S TERRESTRIAL CARNIVORES.

Fred Bruemmer/Valan Photos

ABOVE: THE POLAR BEAR HAS
HAD TO LEARN PATIENCE IN
ITS PURSUIT OF SEALS, WALRUS
CALVES AND OTHER MARINE
LIFE; IT HAS ALSO LEARNED
SOMETHING ABOUT BEING ON
GUARD AGAINST ADULT MALES
FROM ITS MOTHER, OPPOSITE
PAGE, FAR RIGHT, AND ABOUT
PLAYFUL FISTICUFFS FROM ITS
SIBLINGS, OPPOSITE PAGE,
NEAR RIGHT.

For a creature accustomed to consuming more than 150 lbs. of blubber at a winter sitting, this meager fare inevitably produces a marked decrease in energy.

The polar bear is partial to walrus calves, although adult walruses are among its chief nemeses. The bear's favorite tactic in this quest is to charge into a basking herd, then take any calf stalled in the confusion. Also, polar bears seem to know that certain ducks—especially eiders and scoters—dive when they are frightened, so when mammal food is not available, they will submerge themselves to go after the waterfowl.

Aside from the walrus, the polar bear's principal predators are killer whales and hunters. Eskimos use their skins for clothing and their meat and blubber for food. The liver of a polar bear is, however, extremely toxic to humans, containing almost 25,000 units of vitamin A per gram. This can cause nausea, headaches, temporary blindness and even death. Polar bears are also particularly susceptible to the parasitic worm *Trichinella*.

SOCIALIZATION

Some recent studies have questioned the long-held view that polar bears are solitary in their general social behavior. Indeed, some researchers have reported cases of male bears maintaining "friendships" for years as they wander across the ice pack. Polar bears are

also more playful than once thought, as typi-
fied in this description by Fred Bruemmer in
a December 1984 article published by *Natural History* magazine:

> *One places a . . . paw upon the other's
> shoulder, they rise and spar and push,
> lose balance and embrace, sway and
> wrestle. One topples and lies on his back,
> huge paws pedaling in the air. The other,
> jaws agape, throws himself on top and
> they romp on the ground, then rise and
> wrestle again. Considering their awesome
> power, the bears practice marvelous re-
> straint and are extremely careful not to
> hurt one another.*

None of this is to suggest that polar bears
have pack tendencies; on the contrary, aside
from play sightings such as the one reported
by Bruemmer, their major initiatives in sociability are in occasional charges of a walrus
herd and the devouring of a whale carcass—
group actions prompted more by coincidental
arrivals on the scene than by cooperative
strategies.

REPRODUCTION

Most polar bears reach their sexual maturity
between five and seven years of age. The mating season for polar bears consists of a brief
encounter of two weeks in April or May during
the female's fertile period. The delayed implantation process allows the fertilized egg to
lie dormant until some time in October, when
the mother has completed the migration back
north to its winter den in a snowbank or ice
ridge. On average, three cubs will be born in
late December or early January; each cub
weighs less than 2 lbs., is hairless, sightless
and scarcely able to maintain its own body
heat. By suckling on their mother's fat-rich
milk, however, the cubs will weigh about
20 lbs. each when they are big enough to
emerge from their den in March.

During their first spring, the cubs will remain close to their mothers; like other bears,
they face particular danger from adult males
and walruses during this period. The mothers

swim through the broken ice with the cubs on their backs, or tow them by the tail, as they teach them to hunt and fish. Until they are almost two years old, the cubs will continue to suckle up to seven times a day, but long before that—usually by the middle of their first summer—they will have acquired a taste for seal blood and fat and will have grown to 100 lbs. In most cases, the family unit will stay together through the next winter and into a second spring, when the mother, again entering estrus, will drive the cubs away. However, there are recorded exceptions of cubs that remain close to their mothers for as long as four winters.

By the time they are off fending for themselves, the young bears weigh about 200 lbs., but they still are nowhere near their average adult weight. Among their more immediate acclimation lessons is staying away from adult males and walruses. Their average longevity in the wild remains a source of dispute, but captive polar bears have lived as long as thirty-five years.

POLAR BEARS BEGIN THEIR ITINERANT WAYS AT A VERY EARLY AGE.

HIBERNATION

Although the hibernation of polar bears generally follows the system of the genus as a whole, there are some distinctions. First, the fat that sustains polar bears during the winter is, strictly speaking, not their own, but that of seals. Second, while females will normally hibernate through the polar night, males are more restless, in some instances going to ground only for a couple of weeks. Third, the

frequently violent winds of the arctic regions cause many lairs to become unsuitable in the midst of hibernation, forcing the bears to move to other quarters. These new quarters are, for the most part, dens abandoned by other bears for similar reasons.

Researchers have identified some seventeen significant denning sites over the circumpolar range of the polar bear. The most populous of these—each with an estimated 150 lairs—are thought to be in Franz Josef Land, on Wrangel Island (off the northeasternmost tip of Siberia), and about 40 mi. south of Churchill, Manitoba. The Churchill area also hosts numerous summer dens that have been dug down through the tundra to permafrost and have apparently been used for hundreds of years by overheated bears seeking cool retreats during these hotter months, particularly in July and August.

CHAPTER

7

THE BEAR
AS EMBLEM

States, regions, cities, private companies and professional organizations around the world have adopted the bear as a symbol of their endeavors and aspirations. For the most part, the animal's emblematic appeal has been its noted strength and sturdiness; in other cases, local traditions and folk stories have accounted for its representational significance.

CIVIC EMBLEMS

The only nation identified with the bear in the modern era—the Soviet Union—could have done without the distinction. The symbol appeared originally in a series of cartoons published by the British periodical *Punch* in February 1878 to back editorial charges that Czarist Russia was bent on an aggressive political course with its European neighbors. The negative connotations persisted through the twentieth century, with Western cartoonists usually contrasting the rapacious Soviet bear to the noble American eagle or valiant British lion. The Soviets themselves showed little fondness for the symbol—at least until the 1980 Olympics in Moscow, when they bowed to the popular perception, but also outflanked their critics by making the decidedly benign bear Misha the official symbol of the international games.

In the United States, bears have emblematic connections to six states. Most prominently, California has made the grizzly bear the official state animal and incorporated it into the state seal. In addition, the bear is configured in the state flag as an evocation of the Bear Republic, the banner under which

Sonoma settlers rebelled against Mexican rule on June 14, 1846. But for all that, California is not the Bear State; that epithet belongs to Arkansas, where in frontier days the bear was a hunting staple.

For much of the nineteenth century, Kentucky was also known as the Bear State because of the large bear population within the territory. At one time, it was also common to refer to Kentuckians as Bears, much in the way that natives of Indiana are called Hoosiers.

New Mexico's adoption of the bear as its official animal occurred in 1963 along with a campaign by the state's game and fisheries department to save the black bear from extinction. Also in New Mexico, in the Lincoln National Forest, a black bear cub was saved during a 1944 forest fire; this animal eventually inspired the famous Smokey the Bear fire-prevention posters. West Virginia also adopted the bear as its state animal in 1955 after a poll conducted of the state's schoolchildren.

WORDS AND EXPRESSIONS

In one language or another, prompted by one perceived attribute or another, the bear has spawned a hefty dictionary of everyday words. In English, they include derivatives from the Teutonic stem *ber-*, such as beer, barley, barn, berth, berate, bier, bereave and berg, but also such cognates as iron, feral, fertile and ferocious.

The word *bear* in itself has more than forty distinct meanings in English, making it one of the most versatile terms in the language. Among its meanings are to bring forth or produce; to support; to maintain; to be susceptible to; to orient; to be relevant; to forge; to be accountable; to tolerate; to convey; to possess; to confirm; and to remember.

Of the numerous expressions and idioms related to the animal, one of the most familiar is the "bear," the stock-exchange idiom for a speculator who sells a stock not actually in his possession in the belief that before he has to deliver the stock to its purchaser, its price will drop, enabling him to profit from the transaction. The expression appears to have originated from the American frontier proverb of "selling the bear's skin before the bear has been caught."

Since 1822, Missouri's official seal has included three bears. Designed by Judge Robert William Wells, the seal shows the two larger silvertips holding up the state motto, UNITED WE STAND DIVIDED WE FALL, to suggest that, while inhabitants are capable of supporting themselves by their internal strength, they also endorse the federal government. The third bear, a grizzly, is depicted within the seal itself.

It is curious that all six states that have identified themselves with bears had a somewhat violent history around their entry into the union; of the other forty-four states, on the other hand, only South Dakota, with its coyote emblem, has embraced a mammal of any appreciable size and carnivorous appetite.

Numerous European cities and provinces also feature bears on their flags and standards. For example, the bear has been a charge in Berlin's municipal coat of arms since 1200. In Switzerland, the bear has been a charge in the coat of arms of both the city and the canton of Bern since 1200; the bear has also appeared as charges in the coats of arms of the cantons of Appenzell-Innerrhoden and Appenzell-Ausserrhoden since 1200, presumed to have been inspired by the alleged taming of a bear by St. Gall in the area. In the Royal Arms Flag of Denmark, the great white polar bear symbolizes the Danish territory of Greenland, which has had the animal as an emblem since the seventeenth century. In the Polish city of Przemysl, the bear has been a charge on the coat of arms since the fourteenth century. And farther east, in the Soviet Union, the bear has been a charge on Novgorod's standard since 1781. In Spain, the bear has been a part of Madrid's official stem since the sixteenth century.

Numerous cities and regions, including Berlin and Bern, derive their name from the Teutonic stem *ber-* and its cognate extensions, which mean "bear." Among these are Bergen, Verona, and Bayern (Bavaria). Arctic regions are so named after the Greek word for the animal, *arktos*.

Courtesy of Swiss Tourist Office

THE TEDDY BEAR

Courtesy of Gund, Inc.

The most pervasive commercial exploitation of the bear is undoubtedly the teddy bear, the cuddly toy animal that children around the world have adored for the better part of the twentieth century. Morris Michtom, a Brooklyn, New York, toy manufacturer, created the teddy bear after a highly publicized incident in November 1902 that involved then-president Theodore Roosevelt.

Roosevelt, in Mississippi to resolve a boundary dispute between that state and Louisiana, took time off and went hunting. On his hunting trip, he encountered a bear cub but refused to shoot it. *Washington Star* cartoonist Clifford Berryman, viewing the episode as a fitting metaphor for the president's political mission, came up with a cartoon entitled ''Drawing the Line in Mississippi,'' showing the president turning his back on the cub, that was syndicated from coast to coast.

Seeing the cartoon gave Michtom an idea for a stuffed toy. He made a prototype of a stuffed bear and sold it immediately in his Brooklyn candy store. He then made another stuffed bear and wrote to Roosevelt to get permission to market the item under the president's nickname. Roosevelt's permission granted, Michtom entered into a manufacturing-distribution deal with a company that later became the Ideal Toy Corporation.

Although several other interests in both the United States and Europe have lodged claims to originating the teddy bear, most circumstantial evidence, including correspondence between the Michtom family and Roosevelt, indicates that the Russian immigrant in Brooklyn was its true father.

In many instances, municipal emblems were based on military, clan and aristocratic family symbols. In England and Scotland, for example, the Earldom of Warwick depicts a bear tied to a staff, a fact noted repeatedly by William Shakespeare in *Henry VI*, Part II, especially in Act V, Scene I. Aside from having Warwick himself note that his family crest is "the rampant bear chain'd to the ragged staff," Shakespeare has Young Clifford taunt the arrival of Warwick and the Earl of Salisbury with the words:

> *Are these thy bears? We'll bait thy*
> *bears to death,*
> *And manacle the bear-ward in their*
> *chains. . . .*

Also in the United Kingdom, Sir Herbert Baker, the architect of the Bank of England, designed bear constellations for the bank's floor mosaics as a symbol of the institute's strength in 1694.

The Via dell'Orso, one of Rome's oldest streets, takes its name from a hotel once owned there by Baccio dell'Orso ("Kiss of the Bear"). A local anecdote tells of the time that Baccio hired a painter to work up an artful insignia for his establishment. As the story goes, the painter demanded six scudos to

BRUIN AS A FUN MAKER.

ABOVE: AN 1890 CIRCUS POSTER FEATURING THE BEAR. LEFT: THE DANISH COAT OF ARMS.

Photo by E.H. Baynes/American Museum of Natural History

AS IS EVIDENCED BY THE ILLUSTRATIONS ON THESE PAGES, BEARS HAVE BEEN USED TO SELL A VARIETY OF SERVICES AND PRODUCTS.

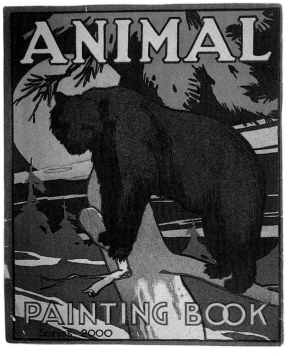

create a representation of two bears standing next to one another, but eight scudos if the bears were to be shown chained together. Opting for the cheaper offer, Baccio was disconcerted a few weeks later when rain completely erased the painter's labors. When he confronted the painter about the transience of his work, the latter was said to have replied: "I warned you to accept the chains. Now, you see, the bears simply ran away."

Another street in Rome, known today as the Via Bibiana, was for many centuries called the Via dell'Orso Pileato ("Street of the Hatted Bear"). Today, the church of Saint Bibiana houses fragments of a statue of a hatted bear that dates back to the fifth century.

ADVERTISING EMBLEMS

At one time or another, entrepreneurs have found the bear a suitable image for commercial products. Thus, the animal has been used to sell lettuce, soap, waterproof clothing, automotive supplies, motel rooms and cookies.

As warrior, divinity or suckling mother, the bear has inspired parents from every continent in the world to give their children names derived from it. Some of the more noted Western names are Orson, Ursula, Bjorn, Robert, Bruno, Herbert, Bertha, Arthur and Bernard.

SPORTS EMBLEMS

Like other animals with prodigious strength, the bear has been appropriated as an emblem by numerous professional and nonprofessional sports teams. In 1924, the bear was adopted as a fitting symbol of the first United States franchise in the National Hockey League, the Boston Bruins. Chicago's football team has been called the Bears since 1922, when owner "Papa Bear" George Halas concluded that

PRODUCE OF U.S.A.
GOLDEN BEAR
CALIFORNIA FRUITS
GROWN AND PACKED BY F.D.WILLIAMSON, MILLS, CALIFORNIA.

the then-named Decatur Staleys needed a more aggressive image for the National Football League. Twenty-three years earlier, in 1899, Chicago changed the name of its baseball team to the Cubs, a moniker very much in tune with an era in which youth and promise were valued as highly as strength.

North American universities have draped bearskins over their athletes in football, baseball, basketball, soccer and other sports. Among these are Brown University's Bruins,

the Black Bears of the University of Maine, the Baylor Bears, the University of California's Golden Bears, the UCLA Bruins, the Bears of the University of Northern Colorado, and the University of Alberta's Golden Bears.

And a Cub Scout is, of course, a youngster apprenticing in the ways of nature before being accepted as a full-fledged Boy Scout. Of the three possible ranks a child can achieve—Bobcat, Wolf and Bear—the Bear is the highest.

CORDIAL CAMPARI
DAVIDE CAMPARI & C. MILANO
STABILIMENTO A SESTO S. GIOVANNI

CHAPTER

8

BLACK
BEARS

Like that of its brown cousin, the coloring of the black bear *(Ursus americanus)* invites much confusion about its name. In fact, black bears are as likely to be cinnamon, beige, white or blue in color as they are black. Not least for this reason, a few researchers have suggested that the animal be given a more rigorously descriptive name, but no one has come up with a suitable replacement yet.

DISTRIBUTION

One better name might be a straight translation of the Latin *Ursus americanus*, meaning American bear, since a black bear is strictly an American mammal. From the arctic tree line down to northern Mexico and from Newfoundland to Western Canada, the black bear inhabits most North American forests of any size and is scarce only in the Great Plains region. Within this vast territory, this bear has shown particular preference for the hardwood forests of the southeastern United States and the coniferous regions of the Pacific Northwest. Since much of their range lies close to heavily populated zones, black bears have had to develop more than the usual ursine social curiosities and defenses where humans are concerned; conversely, their relative conspicuousness has generated more than normal human observation (planned and unplanned) and promoted a widespread conclusion that they have more "personality" than brown and polar bears.

PHYSICAL TRAITS

Whatever their color, black bears are plantigrade, with short, nonretractile claws. Adult males weigh anywhere from 150 to 300 lbs., although a rare few have reached almost 600 lbs., and females usually weigh no more than 150 lbs. Black bears have small eyes, round and erect ears and short tails. A typical black bear grows to be between 5 and 6 ft. long, with a horizontal shoulder-to-rump line. The bear reaches maturity at four years and has a markedly short life span; healthy males generally live no more than five or six years, while females live to an average seven to eight

A TYPICAL BLACK BEAR GROWS TO BETWEEN 5 AND 6 FEET LONG, AND HAS A HORIZONTAL SHOULDER-TO-RUMP LINE.

© Aubrey Lang/Valan Photos

years. There have been, however, many recorded instances of the animals surviving into their teens and even their twenties.

As was the case with the brown bear in the past, the variety of colors among black bears once prompted a belief that the animals belonged to different species; only in this century has a closer examination of skulls, teeth, claws and pelts confirmed a common family.

One of the most striking black bears is the glacial bear of central Alaska and the Yukon, which has a decidedly bluish tinge that makes it difficult to distinguish it from the icy background of its habitat. Recent field studies indicate, however, that this particular variation may be dying out through breeding with bears of other colors.

Even more exotic than the glacial bear is the Kermode bear, which is found in isolated areas of coastal British Columbia. Named for Francis Kermode, a turn-of-the-century Canadian naturalist, the Kermode bear has a cream-colored hide and, from a distance, can be confused with a polar bear. Kermodes can also be reddish, orange, bright yellow or blue-gray in color. In all recorded cases, however, black bears have been found to have brown eyes, which belies a briefly held theory among their earliest discoverers that Kermodes were albinos. Given their esoteric appearance, it is not surprising that Kermodes have inspired a tradition of mystical beliefs among the native peoples of British Columbia, who often refer to black bears as ghost bears.

THE KERMODE BEAR'S UNUSUAL COLORING HAS LED SOME PEOPLE TO CALL IT A GHOST BEAR AND TO ATTRIBUTE IT WITH MYSTICAL QUALITIES.

STREAMS ARE ONLY ONE SOURCE OF SUSTENANCE FOR THE BLACK BEAR, ONE OF THE ANIMAL KINGDOM'S MOST CONSPICUOUS GOURMANDS.

HUNTING AND EATING HABITS

The only thing more diverse than the black bear's colors is its diet; it seems capable of eating just about anything, including a camper's leftovers or the canned goods left in a forest dweller's storehouse. When the bear is hungry enough, it has also been known not to let anything stand between its stomach and a meal—least of all a tree, boulder or trailer door. Some witnesses have even reported cabin walls that were destroyed by black bears intent on getting to the source of aromas on the other side.

Generally speaking, about 75 percent of the black bear's diet comes from vegetable matter; the rest is divided among small mammals, insects, amphibians, birds, fish and eggs. In making the seasonal rounds common to its genus, the black bear will usually concentrate on clover, roots and catkins for the first couple of weeks after it emerges from its winter den. In a successive period, it will focus on rodents, the carrion left by hunters or disease, fruits, flowers and every conceivable kind of berry found in wooded areas. At one time, the eastern United States black bear was considered to be a chestnut connoisseur, but a series of blights to the tree at the beginning of the twentieth century forced it to substitute acorns on its menu. The switch was instructive to researchers for two reasons: the

A BLACK BEAR SPENDS A
GOOD PART OF ITS DAILY
WANDERINGS SMACKING AT
TREE ROOTS AND LOGS IN
SEARCH OF INSECTS.

animal's ability to scale oak trees to get at the acorns dispelled the myth that it was a clumsy climber, and its skill at separating the meat and shell of the acorn demonstrated the fine precision of its claws. Much of the black bear's reputation for fastidiousness also comes from its habit of carefully licking up any acorn meat that drips onto its paws as it cracks open the shell.

The black bear's parallel reputation as a smasher is illustrated by its habit of spending a good part of its daily wanderings smacking at roots and logs in order to get at what lies beneath. As often as not, the bear's prey includes beetles, hornets, grasshoppers and other insects. The animal's legendary encounters with beehives is based very much on fact: it is not unusual for a black bear to crack open more than a half-dozen hives in a day.

As the summer progresses, black bears step up their food intake until they average a daily weight gain of slightly less than 2 lbs. Their fare will depend on the terrain; they eat salmon and moose calves in Alaska, and carrion and lemmings in Northern Canada. The summer is also the animal's period of greatest vulnerability in that its wider foraging and the vacation season make encounters with humans more likely. Not that the bear is completely unable to cope with the situation; to the contrary, it has refined its panhandling skills to an art in state parks, become skilled at pilfering at campsites and, on occasion, learned to overturn small automobiles that have been left parked with food inside. Overall, however, it is usually the bear that comes out the worse for the contact with man, as many bears are shot to defend vacationers.

TERRITORIALITY

Where ranging is concerned, the black bear seems to require only a vegetative cover, being equally at home in temperate or boreal climates, in thorn forests and chaparral, in pine parklands and conifer woods, in swamps and subalpine areas. Depending on food availability, the adult male will range up to 150 sq. mi. and the female up to about 50 sq. mi. The recorded extremes are a male in Pennsylvania that was once tracked for 380 sq. mi.

and a female in Arizona that moved no further than 10 sq. mi. from its winter den.

Black bears mark trees along their ranging route, especially during the summer breeding season. The marking usually consists of bite or claw impressions about 4 or 5 ft. from the ground on deciduous trees. Although the timing and regularity of the markings suggest a connection to the animal's mating season, there has not as yet been a definitive scientific explanation for the ritual.

For the most part, black bears roam at dawn and dusk. If they are having difficulty finding food or if they have an appetite for what man eats, they will take to traveled roadsides during the day or campgrounds at night. Like other bears, black bears have a network of temporary bed sites along their ranging route; most of these sites are little more than shallow depressions in leaf litter that give the bears a commanding view of their surroundings. When the bears are more in the mood to avoid human company than to sneak into its food, they will use tree-covered stream beds for a path. Although capable of moving as fast as 30 mi. an hour, black bears seldom run; if imperiled by human hunters or larger mammals, they will generally scamper up a tree for safety.

The black bear's readiness to enter human communities in search of food was at one time considered something of a contradiction for a mammal generally viewed as far less aggressive than the grizzly and other American brown bears. But more extensive observation in recent decades has portrayed the black bear as far more calculating than timid and in possession of an elaborate sensory network that it relies on for staying out of conflict in threatening situations. Signs that the black

bear is reacting are general body posturing, ear position, bowed head, low moan vocalization and blow vocalization coupled with an extension of the lips. One 1980 study of black bears in the Great Smoky Mountains National Park recorded 624 aggressive acts by bears toward human beings, of which only thirty-seven (5.9 percent) resulted in actual contact. Many experts believe that the dense woodlands that are home to most black bears make them feel safe, so they have a more calibrated tolerance toward humans than brown bears and polar bears, which are relatively more vulnerable in their respective habitats.

REPRODUCTION

The mating season for black bears varies
from climate to climate; most breeding in the
south starts in May, but often does not begin
in the north before late July or August. Also
because of temperature factors, the female's
age of sexual maturity can vacillate from an
uncommon two years to an occasional seven
years; between three and four years is normal.
Although there is no definite proof of this, the
further north a female bear lives, the older it
seems to be when it reaches estrus.

Mating among black bears is similar to
that of dogs, lasts from fifteen to thirty minutes
and occurs several times over a two- to three-
week period. Delayed implantation occurs
between late November and early December;
cubs are born two months later, between the
end of January and the beginning of February.
The normal litter size is two, but it is not uncommon for a female to have three or four
cubs. At birth, the hairless, sightless infants
weigh no more than 12 oz.

Black bear cubs are second to none in
general obstreperousness. For the first two
months after birth in their winter den, they
feed exclusively off the high-protein, high-fat
milk of the mother; feeding occurs several

**BECAUSE OF HUMAN
ENCROACHMENTS, BLACK
BEARS NOW LARGELY CONFINE
THEIR TRAVELING TO DAWN
AND DUSK.**

DESPITE THEIR CUTE APPEARANCE, BLACK BEAR CUBS HAVE GAINED A REPUTATION AS BEING WITHOUT EQUAL FOR GENERAL UNRULINESS.

times a day and is a noisy crescendo of screeches, growls and whimpers. Weighing close to 20 lbs. when they emerge from the winter lair, the cubs are immediately into everything—digging, mouthing and pawing at the ground, trees and each other. All bear cubs spend a good part of their first summer playing and play-fighting with one another, but the small black bears go at their games with particular energy, which often leads to regular interventions from a fearful mother. But the intervening mother might often be smarter to leave her cubs alone, because when they aren't scuffling among themselves and wreaking havoc on their terrain, they are clinging to or clawing at her with an almost-desperate need for nurturing and comfort. Zoologists experienced with both wild and captive black cubs have been hard-pressed not to drag out words like loutish, bratty and tyrannical to describe them.

However, the lot of the cubs is not all self-ish. Up to an average 70 lbs. by the end of their first summer, they reap the benefits of

another winter with the mother, but then, the following summer, when they have reached more than a couple of hundred pounds, the cubs are left to fend for themselves. Often, the mother will send them up a tree before she wanders off for the last time. At that point, the dangers that the cubs had faced earlier with male bears, pumas and wolves become even more acute. One authoritative estimate is that about one-fourth of black bear cubs are killed during their first year, and another one-third die in the period immediately following their abandonment. The cubs' unfamiliarity with areas beyond the mother's range, combined with their rambunctiousness, results in many of them being shot by farmers and ranchers as nuisances.

SOCIALIZATION

Except for mothers in the company of their cubs, black bears are normally solitary travelers. But given that premise, their sociability seems more sophisticated than that of brown bears or polar bears. While polar bears tolerate each other in cases of sudden food windfalls like a herd of seals, black bears tolerate the proximity of rivals even in their individual grazings. This is not to say that adult males, in particular, don't fight when they feel challenged: they do fight, and often. However, the caprices of their food supply and the elaborateness of their defense signals make it possible for them to forage near one another without obsessive concern.

HIBERNATION

The black bear's denning routine depends on latitude, available food, weather conditions and the sex and age of the particular animal. In general, adult females go to ground first, followed by adult males, then subadult males

© Leonard Lee Rue III/FPG International

and females. In the northernmost areas of the bear's American domain, the den is likely to be a snow-covered culvert or cave that is entered in mid-October. Further south, denning will not begin until well into November or even mid-December; here, the bear's den could be anything from a depression under a boulder to a log. In Louisiana and other states in the Deep South, black males will not hibernate in any real sense at all: at most they use some protected spot as nightly quarters. What is relatively common to all the dens, regardless of region, is the pregnant female's shrewd exploitation of its smaller size to build lair entrances that are too tight for any marauding male to enter. The payback for this is that within a few months the female will have to put up with its demanding cubs.

STUDIES IN RECENT YEARS HAVE CONCLUDED THAT BLACK BEARS ARE LESS SHY AND MORE CALCULATING THAN THEIR BROWN BEAR COUSINS WHEN IT COMES TO DEALING WITH HUMANS.

CHAPTER

9

OTHER
BEARS

Selenarctos thibetanus

Of the other five bear species, four (the moon bear, sun bear, sloth bear and giant panda) are indigenous to Asia, one (the spectacled bear) to South America. Because of a combination of geographical, historical and political factors, significantly less is known about these members of the Ursidae family than about brown, polar and black bears.

What has become increasingly clear about all five animals, however, is that they face greater extinction threats than the more noted species.

MOON BEAR

The most imposing looking of the other five bears is undoubtedly *Selenarctos thibetanus*, which literally means "moon bear of Tibet." This bear is referred to at times as the Tibetan black bear, the Himalayan black bear or the Asiatic black bear. The moon association stems from a large crescent-shaped mark on the animal's chest; sometimes the mark is white, yellow or even orange-yellow.

While the moon bear is at home in the Himalayas, the growing tendency to refer to it only as the moon bear indicates how common it is to other parts of Asia as well. In fact, after

resolving decades of debate about whether the moon bear was the same species in all cases, scientists now can trace the moon bear west from the Tibetan Plateau to northern Pakistan, southern parts of the Soviet Union, Afghanistan and Iran; north to Manchuria and other forested zones of China; south to Bangladesh and the Indian state of Assam; and southeast to Laos. The animal can also be found in Taiwan and on the Japanese islands of Honshu and Shikoku.

Aside from its chest marking, the moon bear is distinguished by a soft, shaggy pelt that is normally glossy black in color but is sometimes closer to dark brown. Younger bears have a brown or tan muzzle that grows white as the animals age; the upper lip and chin also grow hoarier with age. The length of the bear's hair depends on its food and fat intake; a manelike ruff around the shoulders is a sign of a plentiful diet. The moon bear's head is blunt, and its short, rounded ears are set far apart. The bear has short front claws adapted for climbing, and its legs are notably more slender than those of its cousins. The average moon bear is slightly less than 6 ft. long and weighs about 250 lbs., although some have topped 400 lbs. As is the case with all bears, the males are about one-fourth to one-third larger than the females.

As a rule, moon bears are guided by their chest marking insofar as they sleep in caves or hollow trees for most of the day and go foraging when the sun sets. Their diet consists mainly of insects, fruit and plant materials, and they will climb rather high to get at cherries, nuts and berries. Although a moon bear's meat eating is largely restricted to carrion, lack of other edibles in some areas of Tibet and in Assam have made sheep, goats and

cattle frequent prey. Fish are not on the animal's menu.

The most extensive study of the moon bear's eating habits was conducted in Japan, where the havoc the animal wreaks on trees has become a justification for widespread hunting of the creature. Despite some initial attempts to distract the bear with other edibles, it persists, especially in the summer months, in not only peeling away the bark from the trees it comes across, but also in gnawing away at the exposed sapwood. It is not uncommon for the animal to destroy as many as forty trees in one night. Making matters even worse is the fact that its favorite targets are Japanese cypresses and Japanese cedars, bulwarks of the country's timber industry. In the name of economic survival, lumbermen and hunters have been killing an estimated 2,500 bears annually in recent years. Partly as a result of such hunting and partly because of general industrial expansion, the moon bear has practically disappeared from the Japanese island of Kyushu, where it was once a fairly common presence.

FOR POACHERS, THE MOON BEAR'S HABIT OF WREAKING HAVOC ON TREES HAS JUSTIFIED HUNTING THE ANIMAL.

The denning routine of moon bears varies with climate. In the most temperate zones, adult males might eschew hibernation altogether; in colder regions, they will uphold the traditional retreat to snow-covered dens from November to March or early April. Only pregnant females always observe the customary ursine cycle. As for the dens themselves, the bears have shown a particular fondness for the rotten centers of hollow trees like the linden and sometimes dig in as high as 60 ft. off the ground. Caves and dugouts beneath tree roots are alternative lairs. Like brown bears, denning moon bears prevent themselves from defecating during this period with a clot of hair and vegetable material.

Relatively little is known for certain about the moon bear's reproductive calendar, but the evidence on hand suggests that, like other bears, its mating season depends upon climate. For this bear, a temperate region permits breeding at any time from April to November, while a colder environment dictates summer coupling. Normal gestation runs between seven and eight months in line with delayed implantation. A typical moon bear litter is two cubs, each weighing about 8 oz. The cubs open their eyes a week after birth; they are able to accompany their mother on foraging expeditions about one month later. Unlike other species, moon bear cubs have been known to remain with their parent even after the standard eighteen to twenty months; witnesses in Japan and the Himalayas have reported females on the prowl with two sets of cubs.

Some moon bears have survived in captivity until past the age of thirty, but the growing forces against them in the wild will soon make this a very rare exception. Besides the threat

posed by hunters and lumberjacks in Japan, the species faces devastation from the Chinese, who favor their paws as a food delicacy; from the Chinese, Laotians and Taiwanese, who believe their bile and bones have medicinal properties; and from Indians, Pakistanis and Afghans, who shoot mother bears to capture cubs for training as carnival and marketplace performers. On May 1, 1990, the *New York Times* cited a report issued by the U.S. Fish and Wildlife Service that warned that the moon bear "could become extinct throughout much of its range in the near future . . . unless steps are taken to reduce the extensive trafficking in bear parts and to manage hunting."

SUN BEAR

The sun bear *(Helarctos malayanus)*, the smallest member of the Ursidae family, inhabits the dense tropical forests of northeast India, Burma, southern China, Thailand and Malaysia, and the Indonesian provinces of Borneo and Sumatra. Sometimes called a honey bear or a Malay bear, it weighs an average of 100 lbs. and is 4 ft. in length when an adult. Basically black, most sun bears have a

white or yellow chest marking that accounts for their association with the sun. Its head is usually short and flat, its muzzle may be gray, orange or a combination of both colors, its ears are small and rounded and its eyes are decidedly beady. The bear also has some bizarre whorls and cowlicks on its forehead and behind its ears. The most arboreal member of the bear family, the sun bear has a bandy-legged, ungainly way of moving on the ground, but uses its sicklelike claws to scale trees with very little effort.

The sun bear is mostly vegetarian. While it favors mushrooms, honey, fruit and insects, it won't pass up lizards and rodents that cross its path. For all its herbivorous ways, the sun bear has a reputation for being one of the most ferocious animals in the jungle and will rarely hesitate to use its sharp claws and powerful jaws on any larger mammal that threatens it. Countless stories of Indian and Indonesian villagers say the bear will charge humans without cause. When grabbed by a tiger or some other large predator, the sun bear can wriggle its body far enough under its loose pelt to be able to turn back and bite its attacker in the face. In captivity, the animal will spend whole days grunting and roaring as it tears apart any partition not specially reinforced for containing it.

Sun bears spend most of the day sleeping and sunbathing in trees, sometimes as high as 20 ft. off the ground. Their nests are usually platforms of broken branches and resemble those built by orangutans. Sun bears usually forage at night, often in the company of another bear.

At least part of the sun bear's increasingly urgent survival problem is rooted in the same habit that has brought crisis to the moon

© Joe McDonald/Visuals Unlimited

Helarctos

malayanus

THE SUN BEAR SPENDS A GOOD PART OF ITS DAY SUNBATHING IN TREES.

© A.D. Copley/Visuals Unlimited

TOP: MATING FOR THE SUN BEAR IS A PARTICULARLY NOISY AFFAIR, AND INVOLVES BARKING, HUMMING, HUGGING, MOCK FIGHTING AND KISSING. BOTTOM: LIKE THE MOON BEAR, THE SUN BEAR'S RAVENOUS DEPENDENCE ON TREES HAS ALSO MADE IT THE PREY OF HUNTERS, AND CONSEQUENTLY THREATENED ITS EXISTENCE.

the major reasons that the International Union for the Conservation of Nature and the World Wildlife Fund declared sun bears an endangered species in 1978.

Female sun bears reach sexual maturity in their third year. Mating, which can last from a couple of times a day anywhere from a few days to a week at any time of the year, is a particularly noisy affair, and involves barking, humming, hugging, mock fighting and kissing. Without the need for delayed implantation or hibernation in its subtropical climate, the mother sun bear gives birth on average to two cubs about a hundred days after impregnation, usually in a well-protected area of the forest floor. Even more frail than other infant bears, the sun cubs weigh no more than 9 oz. and are about 7 in. long. For the first two weeks of their existence, they neither hear nor see, and have nearly transparent skin. They will not walk for two months and will not be weaned for four. The cubs are so fragile in the first months that the mother licks them to bring on urination and defecation.

bear—the destruction of valuable timber. The sun bear has shown a particular taste for the buds at the top of coconut palms, which are the hearts of the trees. In just a few nights, a single bear can destroy an entire plantation by indulging this preference, which inevitably has caused a massive hunting campaign in many countries. Jacklighting poachers (unauthorized hunters who use automobile headlights or other lamps to blind the animal so they can shoot it easily) are another one of

© Gerry Ellis/The Wildlife Collection

© Joe McDonald/Visuals Unlimited

SLOTH BEAR

For some years, the sloth bear *(Melursus ursinus)* was known in Europe as a bear sloth because hunters in India mistakenly concluded that the animal's arboreal habits made it a relation of the South American sloth. It was only at the beginning of the nineteenth century, when the first live specimen was shipped to a zoo in France, that scientists took a closer look, realized that the animal was a bear and simply switched the order of its first and last names.

Sometimes also called the lip bear, the sloth bear is indigenous to India, Sri Lanka and parts of Nepal. Although this bear rarely grows to weigh more than 250 lbs. and to slightly less than 6 ft. in length, its extremely shaggy black coat and imposing ruff around its neck and shoulders make it appear bigger to the first-time observer. Further enhancing its pelt are a nearly bare belly and underlegs, adaptations that apparently make the bear cooler in its subtropical Indian and Ceylonese ranges. Like other Asian bears, sloth bears have yellow or white chest markings, most often in the shape of a Y, but sometimes closer to a V. Their ivory claws are blunt, curved and about 3 in. long.

The most distinctive feature of the sloth bear is its face. The bear has a muzzle that

Melursus ursinus

THE MOST DISTINCTIVE BUT CERTAINLY NOT THE MOST ATTRACTIVE FEATURE OF THE SLOTH BEAR IS ITS FACE.

THERE IS SOME THOUGHT THAT THE SLOTH BEAR'S LACK OF SIGNIFICANT FACIAL HAIR IS AN ADAPTATION TO PROTECT IT AGAINST THE STICKINESS OF THE TERMITES IT HUNTS WITH REGULARITY.

varies between dirty white and gray, extremely protrusible lips, nostrils that can be opened and closed at will, few molar teeth, no front teeth at all and a hollowed out, bony palate. The mouth modifications in particular have made the bear very much a bête noire for forest termites, which are the animal's principal dietary item. Some naturalists have also speculated that the lack of significant hair on the bear's face is another specific adaptation to protect it against the sticky secretions of termites under attack.

A sloth bear feeding on termites can be one of the more obnoxious sights of jungle dining. To set its table, the sloth bear will smash into a termite mound or a rotten log where it expects to find a colony. Once it has ripped aside the outer parts of the structure, the bear will pucker up and blow violently to drive away dust and other materials that might taint its edibles. Finally, it will begin sucking up the termites and their larvae with an ear-splitting huffing and puffing that can be heard 200 ft. away.

Sloth bears also like ants, honey, berries and crops like maize, yams and sugarcane. Their flesh consumption is generally limited to a carcass already picked relatively clean by another carnivore, particularly tigers. Whether because of their insect and honey intake or some other metabolic factor, the bears drink water regularly, more than most animals do, in the hottest months.

Most of the sloth bear's foraging takes place after dusk. At this time, the bear is normally so intent on its prey that it grows careless about humans and other mammals happening by, which is somewhat atypical for the genus. In such cases, however, it is generally the intruder that pays for the encounter; the startled bear instinctively responds with a roaring defense that almost always includes bluff charges, growling while standing erect and, sometimes, vicious maulings. When they decide to withdraw, the bears will abandon their usual shambling gait for a gallop. But despite their climbing talents, they seldom take to trees in order to elude enemies.

Selected study of the sloth bear in Nepal's Royal Chitwan National Park suggests a distribution of one animal every 10 sq. mi. Because termites and ants are rather plentiful in its ranging zones, the sloth bear rarely encounters food supply problems, and thus has less reason than other bears to congregate in feeding groups around some urgently needed prey. Whether it is because the sloth bear has less cause to worry about competition, or whether it is because it has a gregarious nature, it is among the most sociable members of the bear family. In fact, the sloth bear spends long hours communicating with its fellow bears in an array of roars, squeals, yelps, huffs, puffs and gurgles. Adult males have also been seen foraging together with their families.

The sloth bear's penchant for vocalizing is also very much in evidence during mating, which usually features a great deal of barking, screeching and mock-scuffling. The mating season itself varies with the bear's range: in India, for example, mating seems to take place only between April and June, yet in Sri Lanka, it might occur at any time. Spring matings usually produce litters in December and January, which indicates delayed implantation. The births usually occur in dens that are dug out under boulders or in caves that are otherwise retreated to only during monsoon seasons; it has been determined that the sloth bear does not hibernate.

The average sloth bear litter is two cubs, which are born sightless and remain so for about three weeks. About one week or two after the cubs gain sight, the mother will abandon the den and carry the cubs on its back while it goes off in search of food. Position is everything for the cubs on the mother's flanks, so that a cub that has been assigned to the shoulders will fight to get back to that exact spot if it gets displaced. The mother will put up with its riders until they have grown to about one-third of its size, which is about two-and-a-half years after delivery.

The sloth bear's chief nemeses are wild dogs, tigers and humans. The latter has proven particularly pernicious, not only because of the vast deforestation projects that have threatened the animal's habitat on the Asian subcontinent, but also because of hunters hired to kill the animal by merchants bent on selling its fat as a hair restorer and its penis bone as a magical cure for sexual impotence.

SLOTH BEARS ARE AMONG THE MORE SOCIABLE BEARS.

THE SPECTACLED BEAR GETS ITS NAME FROM THE FACIAL LINES THAT OFTEN CONTRIVE TO MAKE RINGS AROUND ITS EYES, WHICH CREATE THE IMPRESSION OF EYEGLASSES.

© Milton H. Tierney, Jr./Visuals Unlimited

SPECTACLED BEAR

The spectacled or Andean bear *(Tremarctos ornatus)* is the only survivor of the short-faced mammals that roamed across the Americas during the Pleistocene epoch 1.5 million years ago. Besides the popular spectacled bear and Andean bear, the animal has other regional names such as the red-fronted bear, the white-fronted bear, the black puma, the underbark-eating bear and the cow-eating bear. The only bear now living in South America (or in the southern hemisphere anywhere), the spectacled bear can be found in Venezuela and Colombia, in the foothills of Ecuador, Peru and Chile, and in scattered zones of Bolivia. Sporadically reported sightings in Brazil, Argentina and Panama have never received definitive confirmation.

The shaggy, black spectacled bear gets its name from facial lines that often contrive to make rings around its eyes, which create the impression of eyeglasses. Sometimes the markings are yellow or white, as its sun-bearlike chest markings are, or even light red.

Despite its being as arboreal as the sun bear, the spectacled bear is much heavier than its Asian relative. The average adult spectacled bear weighs between 175 and 275 lbs. and is up to 6 ft. long, not counting its 3-in. tail, and 2.5 ft. tall on all fours. Some male specimens have been recorded as weighing as much as 380 lbs. and extending more than 7 ft. long.

Spectacled bears are markedly herbivorous, although shortages in their regular food sources and accessible cattle may make meat account for more than 7 percent of their diet. Preferred edibles include fruit, maize, honey and sugarcane, but the animal's powerful

jaws also allow it to tackle palm nuts, cactus and a wide range of bromeliads that other creatures find too tough to eat. The bromeliads (epiphytes that grow on tree branches) are also an important source of water because of the rain they collect. When the opportunity presents itself, the bear will also go after ants, mice, birds, rabbits and llamas. Attacks on domestic cattle, relatively infrequent as they are, are always considered ominous by ranchers because of the bear's habit of returning repeatedly to the same grazing ground. Unfortunately, the intruding bear is usually shot in these incidents.

Spectacled bears will forage at dawn and dusk when they are in a dense forest, but only at night when they are in more open country. As bears go, spectacled bears are regarded as timid, as they usually travel along ridge lines and deep ravines to avoid humans in lower valleys. However, the bear's shyness has done little to ensure its survival. Of the various projections made of their number in the last few years, the most optimistic estimate is that there are little more than five thousand still living in the wild, while a particularly bleak conjecture is that there are fewer than two thousand. There are about a hundred spectacled bears in captivity in zoos around the world.

As with the sloth bear, the spectacled bear's greatest extinction threats are posed by deforestation and merchants who trade the animal's body parts as miracle cures for human ills (for example, the bear's fat is sold as a remedy for arthritis and rheumatism). Farmers

Tremarctos ornatus

© Aubrey Lang/Valan Photos

THE AVERAGE WEIGHT OF THE SPECTACLED BEAR HAS DROPPED DRASTICALLY DUE TO INBREEDING AND OTHER THREATS TO ITS SURVIVAL.

have also joined the assault in recent years by spraying lethal pesticides over crops that are attractive to the bear. In retreating from such perils, the animal has further worsened its situation through increasing inbreeding. Bears in the deserts of Peru that once weighed up to 440 lbs. and would give birth to two to four cubs now average 85 lbs. and almost never have more than one cub.

Spectacled bears breed in the spring between April and June; periods of gestation last up to eight months. To date, scientists have only been able to speculate about a delayed implantation process at work, but they have been firmer in their conclusions that the births are timed for the December through February period to coincide with the flowering of the South American fruit season. There is no evidence that the spectacled bear is a hibernator, even though most deliveries occur in ground lairs beneath boulders or roots.

The typical litter is two cubs, each one weighing slightly less than 1 lb. The cubs open their eyes between three and four weeks after birth, and a week or so after they can see, they venture forth from the lair. Until they are at least two months old, however, the cubs are more helpless than most newborns and even have to be urged to suckle by the mother. The spectacled bear is also the only bear that will actually carry food to its issue. Throughout the nursing period, vocal communication is constant, with an exchange of various trills, hums and even owllike screechings between the mother and her cubs. Adult males have been seen in the company of families, but little is known about the attitude of other males toward the newborn. The cubs strike out on their own when they are about six months old.

GIANT PANDA

Yes, it is a bear.

Only in the last twenty-five years have scientists marshaled sufficient evidence to make the case that the giant panda *(Ailuropoda melanoleuca)* is a bona fide member of the bear family. While skeptics remain, meticulous studies made of the animal's DNA sequences, chromosomes and protein characteristics have just about repudiated theories that suggest that the giant panda was a member of the raccoon family or that its anatomical features merited individual classification.

Second to no creature as a symbol of the benign nature of the animal kingdom and of the friendliness possible between man and the lower mammals, the giant panda exists today only in small areas along the eastern rim of the Tibetan Plateau, specifically in north-central and southern Sichuan, southern Shanxi and the southern Gansu provinces of west-central China. A one-time population of estimated hundreds of thousands of giant pandas throughout China and Burma has, according to a recent report by the Chinese Forestry Ministry, been reduced to little more than seven hundred animals in the wild and another 120 in zoos worldwide. Half of those bears remaining in the wild live in reserves monitored by the Peking government.

Giant pandas are white, thick-furred animals with black shoulders, chest and limbs. They have black patches around their eyes and ears. Adults weigh between 200 and 230 lbs. and grow to 6 ft. in length. Although males are usually 15 percent larger than females, this distinction is often imperceptible

Ailuropoda melanoleuca

MORE THAN ANY OTHER LAND ANIMAL, THE GIANT PANDA HAS GALVANIZED WORLD ATTENTION AS TO THE EXTINCTION THAT THREATENS MANY OF THE EARTH'S SPECIES.

© Richard Laird/FPG International

ALTHOUGH OFTEN PORTRAYED AS PLAYFUL, PANDAS ACTUALLY SPEND MOST OF THEIR TIME FORAGING AND EATING, AND ARE VERY MUCH CAPTIVES OF THEIR DIGESTIVE TRACTS.

to first-time observers since the markings of the sexes are identical, and their external genitalia are similar. Both males and females have massive skulls and forty-two powerful teeth suited for grinding and crunching bamboo shoots, their principal dietary item.

In terms of basic anatomy alone, pandas differ from other bears in several important respects. First, they have felinelike slit eyes, as opposed to the genus's normally rounded pupils—a feature that has led the Chinese to call them giant cat bears. Second, their hind feet have no heel pads, which means that they do not leave the manlike footprints other bears do. Most unusual of all, the panda's forepaws have extra bony pads on the heels of their thumbs that are capable of independent movement. This sixth digit (actually a radial sesamoid) enables the bear to handle bamboo shoots and leaves. The giant panda also has a horny lining along its esophagus to help it cope with sharp bamboo splinters.

While bamboo is certainly the panda's main fare (a shortage of this woody grass in both the late 1970s and 1984 decimated up to one-fourth of the bear population each

time, according to Chinese researchers), it is frequently supplemented by other tufted grasses, crocuses, irises, fir bark, small mammals, birds, fish and eggs. Based on studies of captive pandas, the animals are also amenable to meat when there is not much else around; in fact, most zoos will give the panda meat extracts or meat powder as a nutritional supplement. Loggers in China have also told stories of panda raids on meat storehouses, particularly when their own efforts have reduced plant alternatives.

Pandas consume up to 30 lbs. of food a day. Because they have a particularly short small intestine, they digest with difficulty, so food is passing through their stomachs and bowels constantly. As Ramona and Desmond Morris observe in their book *Men and Pandas,* this makes the animal something of a slave to its digestive tract:

> The panda waved goodbye to the nimble-minded world of helter-skelter chases, bloated blood feasts, and sprawling catnaps. Instead it has become . . . a manual laborer, toiling endlessly at its repetitive bamboo-picking tasks.

Fortunately for the panda, except for a mysterious attack of premature blooming once or twice a century, bamboo is not only abundant within its territories in China, but renews its shoots annually. This abundance, combined with the animal's relentless feeding, accounts for the panda's limited ranging area—generally between 1.5 and 2.5 sq. mi. Inevitably, such restricted grazing makes for population overlap; it does not make, however, for sociability. George Schaller describes this condition in his groundbreaking *The Giant Pandas of Wolong:*

A panda population consists of several residents, each living within a small stable home range, all or part of which is shared with others. Adult males and females appear to have somewhat different land tenure systems. Although their ranges may overlap, each female spends most of her time within a discrete core area only [75 to 100 acres] in extent. . . . Males occupy greatly overlapping ranges and lack well-defined core areas, spending time within the core areas of females and subadults.

Pandas mark their range through a series of scent stations on trees or boulders along primary travel routes; this habit is more common among males than females. When they do cross one another's paths—a relatively infrequent occurrence despite their close quarters—the encounters are anything but friendly. Rather, as Schaller says, they are "a blend of coolness and violence and . . . noisy—a medley of squeals, yips, chirps, moans, and barks." It is not known to what extent the interaction is based on territorial priority or, alternatively, rank by age or some other factor.

THE CLASSIFICATION CONTROVERSY

Controversy over the proper zoological classification for the giant panda goes back to the middle of the nineteenth century, when a French priest, Armand David, became the first Westerner on record to observe the animal. David, who sent home pelts of pandas shot by Chinese hunters, dubbed his find *Ursus melanoleucas* (the black-and-white bear).

It was not until 1936, when European and American scientists first saw a living panda, that doubts were raised about David's classification. After comparing all the differences between pandas and other bears—the bamboo diet, minimal carnivorous appetite, failure to hibernate, vocalizations that tended more toward bleats than roars and so on—the researchers concluded that the animal was a close relative of the small red panda *(Ailurus fulgens)*. The small red panda is a foxlike nocturnal mammal indigenous to Nepal, Burma and China and is a part of the raccoon family.

Researchers believed that the giant panda was a part of the raccoon family until 1964, when D. Dwight Davis published evidence (in *The Giant Panda: A Morphological Study of Evolutionary Mechanisms*) that the giant panda's ties to the red panda and the raccoon were almost as primitively evolutionary as those of bears in general to their canine forebears. "Every morphological feature examined," Davis declared, "indicates that the giant panda is nothing more than a highly specialized bear."

Still, some skeptics remained, including some who decided that the giant panda was indeed so highly specialized that it ought to be placed in a classification all its own. Then, in the 1970s and 1980s, molecular biologists went to work in Washington and London and, following a series of elaborate serological and chromosomal tests, sided with Davis. The general conclusion was that, while there was indeed a rudimentary chromosomal link between the panda and the raccoon, their individual families split off from their common ancestor between twenty and forty million years ago, producing separate evolutionary lines. As for the differences between the pandas and other bears, they were ascribed to the environment that compelled the giant panda to rely on bamboo for its survival.

unknown, but captive pandas have lived to age thirty. Aside from dholes, leopards and the various lethal works of man, the animal's major nemeses are such ailments as lung disease and roundworms.

As they feed off of such low-energy victuals as bamboo, pandas do not accumulate enough fat to hibernate for the winter. Their chief defense against cold and snow is to move to lower elevations where they can continue eating. If winter weather pursues them, they will find shelter in a hollow tree until the worst weather has passed.

Giant pandas are probably the least romantic members of the bear family; coupling may be consummated in as little as thirty seconds. In compensation, the male and female will have sex many times within a very short period: one eyewitness account reported more

WHATEVER THEIR OTHER VIRTUES, GIANT PANDAS ARE ANYTHING BUT ROMANTIC—THEY USUALLY COMPLETE THEIR COUPLINGS IN AS LITTLE AS THIRTY SECONDS.

The panda does most of its ranging in the early morning and at dusk, although its ceaseless appetite will also cause it to forage at other times. Generally, the panda ambles quite deliberately, although it can be forced into a trot (not a gallop, like other bears) if it feels threatened by such traditional enemies as dholes (wild canines) and leopards. The average bear's longevity in the wild is still

than forty copulations within only three hours. The traditional mating position calls for the female to crouch with its head down while the male mounts. Most breeding takes place between mid-March and early May.

Gestation, which appears to involve a modified form of delayed implantation, varies from three-and-a-half to four-and-a-half months, with births usually taking place in a cave or in a tree hollow between late August and September. More often than with other bears, the litter will be a single cub, which is just as well, since the mother shows the ability to deal only with one issue and abandons any others without trying to nurture them.

Panda cubs are helpless. At birth, they are abnormally small (only 3 to 5 oz. and 6 in. long), sightless, toothless and so peltless that they are pink. For the first three weeks of life, the surviving cub is cradled continuously by the mother. When the mother goes walking, it will hold the infant against its breast and walk on three legs. Lactation takes place with the mother sitting erect and feeding its offspring as a human mother would.

The cubs begin to take on their fur in their second week of life and white-and-black patterns by the end of their first month. It will be almost two months, however, before they begin to see, and an additional six weeks until they learn to crawl. With their systems finally in place at six months, they begin eating bamboo; by nine months the cubs are fully weaned. Most cubs are a solid 75 or 85 lbs. by their first birthday, but they usually remain with their mothers for another six months before going on their own.

In their first years, giant pandas are much livelier than their heavy bodies suggest they would be. They bathe often, swim for long

ALTHOUGH THE PANDA'S LONGEVITY IN THE WILD IS STILL UNKNOWN, CAPTIVE PANDAS HAVE LIVED TO AGE THIRTY.

stretches of time and like to climb trees, but always descending rump first. It is only as they grow older that their pleasures become more sedentary. Then, they lounge in the sun between feedings like cats; or, as the Chinese would say, like giant cat bears.

It would be difficult to exaggerate the extinction threat that confronts giant pandas. Relentlessly shrinking forest areas have driven the animals into increasingly claustrophobic communities; this isolation, in turn, has augmented the possibilities for genetic inbreeding. Although Chinese authorities have been engaged in conservation efforts for almost twenty-five years, including a death penalty provision for convicted poachers, fears persist that the moves are too small and too late. On the other hand, hopes for the panda's survival have been raised by successful artificial insemination experiments with captured animals. In fact, while a great deal of publicity has been given in recent years to the anguishing failures of pandas like the Washington National Zoo's Ling-Ling to procreate, more than fifty litters have been born in China and elsewhere through artificial insemination with a success rate of about 70 percent. What remains to be seen is whether the animals created with the intervention of humans will themselves foster further generations.

THE KOALA IS NOT A BEAR

© Kenneth Garrett/FPG International

While classifying the giant panda as a bear has required true scientific labor, no such effort is required for ascertaining the zoological status of the koala. The so-called Australian bear is an arboreal marsupial that seems to have acquired its fictitious bear reputation from its generally cublike facial appearance and a pandalike reliance on the shoots of one particular plant (the eucalyptus).

WHAT TO DO IF
YOU MEET A BEAR

Almost everyone is familiar with the fictitious character Goldilocks, who not
only dallied safely in the home of three bears,
but also helped herself to their food and slept
in their beds. Unfortunately, not too many
fables have been written about those who
sought to follow her example.

Where human encounters with bears are
concerned, however, Goldilocks is not the
most dangerous role model. That distinction
belongs to hikers and campers who set off on
their adventures believing that bears will run
away rather than attack humans, that bears
respond to human intrusions in the same way

no matter their genus, and that, even in the
unlikely chance of an attack, bears will be
satisfied to devour the food of the trekker they
encounter. The operative word for every one
of these convictions is half-truth.

The starting point for any discussion of
what to do, and what not to do, when confronted by bears in the wild, is common sense.
Obviously, it would not be smart to compete
with them for beehives, slap salmon out of
their paws or insist on being present to video-
tape the birth of their cubs. But beyond im-
plicit considerations like these, you should
keep in mind that bears do not read the litera-

WARNING

GRIZZLY FREQUENTING AREA TRAVERSED BY THIS TRAIL

BE ALERT

REMOVAL OF THIS SIGN MAY RESULT IN INJURY TO OTHERS

© Jeff Foott/Tom Stack & Associates

ture identifying their characteristics; they are not any more comfortable meeting members of the Sierra Club than they are meeting members of the Kill-the-Grizzly Club. Of course, bears also have a more liberal definition of food than most humans have. In short, it is important to remember that bears in the wild are very wild bears.

To accent the positive first, it is indeed true that, as a general rule, a hiking excursion is safer than driving an automobile. The Alaska Department of Fish and Game has estimated that the car risk is fifty times higher. It is also true, generally speaking, that bears prefer to be left alone and will make an effort to avoid contact with humans trespassing on their territory. As well, there is every evidence that, faced with a choice of a few pounds of chopped steak in a canvas bag and the owner of the bag, bears will opt for the former. But the more ignorant the wayfarer is about some of the peculiarities of man-bear relations, the more likely it is that he or she will be the exception to these general truths.

Until relatively recently, the main cause of disastrous encounters between a wild bear and man was surprise—the animal feeling threatened by some abrupt intrusion into its range and immediately going on the offensive. To avoid this, knowledgeable hikers have traditionally tied bells to their bootlaces, blown horns or simply let out periodic shouts to underline their presence. Additionally, the very conversation of hikers traveling in large groups tends to send bears in the vicinity scampering. In the same vein, the smart hiker, whether alone or in a large group, will leave his dog at home: an unleashed pet that surprises a bear will undoubtedly be attacked.

Avoiding surprise meetings should also be a consideration when pitching camp. Don't set up a tent next to a stream or lake known to attract bears or bivouac on some spot that is close to, but out of the immediate sightline of, the animal's routine roamings. What the bear does not see, it is more than likely to sense, and will not spend too much time wondering why there is some lurking foreign presence. As for the camp itself, it should be laid out so that any curious bear that wanders in will not feel penned up and have a choice of escape routes once it decides that it can do without human company. Campers should also set up tents an appreciable distance, at least 125 to 150 ft., away from food storage and cooking areas.

Aside from surprise, food is the most frequent cause of ugly encounters with bears. Whether this is because the animal smells the actual supplies being carried by an expedition or because, as has become increasingly the case in recent decades with the relentless constriction of bear ranges by man, the animal has come to identify humans with cheeseburgers, granola and garbage cans. Bears that approach parties in state parks for handouts are among the more mild examples of this confrontation. As the animals become more and more conditioned to this source of victuals, they will usually become equally more aggressive in getting their paws on what they want, whether their object is in a backpack, a tent or an automobile. Most experts believe that an instinctive defense of abandoning the desired food and escaping is, at best, a half solution, since it only encourages the bear to be aggressive. For this reason, bears alert to the success of their aggressive tactics usually end up being shot.

Within camps, food should be kept in bear-proof containers, such as those on sale at Alaska's Denali National Park and a few other protected wildernesses. Many campers have also taken to stringing bags of food, at least 12 ft. off the ground, between trees; the bags should not be hung too close to either tree, as nimble bears will be able to grab them. As for burying supplies, don't forget that bears are extremely able ferreters, so that some slapdash hole is liable to prove less than useful. And remember, food odors *are* food odors, so the camper who has spilled half of his meal on his lap would also be advised to put on some other clothing before turning in for the night.

All bears share such a general aversion to humans that, unwittingly or not, it may be wise to adopt the postures or movements associated with rival bears; for example, lowering one's shoulders in a crouch in order to get a good photograph, or pawing at the air in an attempt to drive off an animal. On the other hand, the genus of the bear in question can often determine the wisdom of a defensive ploy. With grizzlies, it has become generally

accepted that a human cornered by the animal stands the best chance of survival by playing dead and continuing to do so for some time after the bear has lost interest in its inert prey—just in case it is hanging around to allay a lingering suspicion. Playing dead for American black bears, on the other hand, is regarded as the fastest way of becoming a snack, and most experts recommend that the trapped individual stand one's ground with the nearest heavy object in hand. Even this strategy, however, has an important exception; the female black bear is primarily and ferociously concerned with protecting its cubs, so banging pots or making as much of a clamor as possible is considered the best defense when encountering her.

For hikers and campers not eager to confront a bear solely with their ability to distinguish the genus before them, various noise bombs, repellent sprays and other nonlethal deterrents may be purchased from specialized houses; local forestry and natural resources offices should be able to supply information regarding bears in the area and proper deterrents.

THIS ILLUSTRATION MAY SUGGEST OTHERWISE, BUT ALL BEARS SHARE A GENERAL AVERSION TO HUMANS.

Northwind Picture Archives

BIBLIOGRAPHY

Asborjnsen, Peter Christian, and Jorgen Moe, eds. *Norwegian Folk Tales.* New York: Pantheon, 1960.

Bouissac, Paul. *Circuses and Culture.* Bloomington: Indiana University Press, 1976.

Campbell, Joseph. *Historical Atlas of World Mythology.* Vol. 1, *The Way of the Animal Powers.* New York: Harper & Row, 1983.

Carpenter, Rhys. *Folk Tale, Fiction, and Saga in the Homeric Epic.* Berkeley: University of California Press, 1956.

Cirlot, J.E. *A Dictionary of Symbols.* New York: Philosophical Library, 1962.

Clark, Ella. *Indian Legends of the Pacific Northwest.* Berkeley: University of California Press, 1953.

Clébert, Jean-Paul. *The Gypsies.* Middlesex, England: Penguin, 1961.

Collinder, Bjorn. *The Lapps.* Princeton: Princeton University Press, 1949.

Cooper, J.C. *An Illustrated Encyclopedia of Traditional Symbols.* London: Thames and Hudson, 1978.

Crossley-Holland, Kevin, trans. *Beowulf.* New York: Farrar, Straus & Giroux, 1968.

Dasent, George Webbe. *A Collection of Popular Tales from the Norse and North German.* London: Norroena, 1905.

Dioszegi, V., ed. *Popular Beliefs and Folklore Tradition in Siberia.* Bloomington: Indiana University Press, 1968.

Domico, Terry. *Bears of the World.* New York: Facts on File, 1988.

East, Ben. *Bears.* New York: Crown, 1977.

Eliade, Mircea. *Birth and Rebirth.* New York: Harper & Row, 1958.

Ferguson, George Wells. *Signs and Symbols in Christian Art.* New York: Oxford University Press, 1954.

Frazer, James G. *The Golden Bough.* New York: MacMillan, 1951.

Fulghum, W.B. *A Dictionary of Biblical Allusions in English Literature.* New York: Holt, Rinehart and Winston, 1965.

Gimbutas, Marija. *The Goddesses and Gods of Old Europe.* Berkeley: University of California Press, 1982.

Grinnell, George Bird. *Blackfoot Lodge Tales.* Lincoln: University of Nebraska Press, 1962.

Jacobs, Joseph, ed. *The Most Delectable History of Reynard the Fox.* New York: Schocken, 1967.

Kerenyi, C. *The Religion of the Greeks and Romans.* London: Thames and Hudson, 1962.

Klingender, Francis. *Animals in Art and Thought to the End of the Middle Ages.* Cambridge: MIT Press, 1971.

Lathem, Edward Connery, ed. *The Poetry of Robert Frost.* New York: Holt, 1928.

Lindow, John. *Swedish Legends and Folk Tales.* Berkeley: University of California Press, 1978.

MacCana, Proinsias. *Celtic Mythology.* Hamlyn, Middlesex: Newness Books, 1983.

MacCulloch, John A., ed. *The Mythology of All Races.* New York: Cooper Square Publications, 1964.

Morgan, Hal. *Symbols of America.* New York: Penguin, 1986.

Murie, Adolph. *The Grizzlies of Mount McKinley.* Seattle and London: University of Washington Press, 1981.

Philippi, Donald L. *Songs of Gods, Songs of Humans.* Princeton: Princeton University Press, 1979.

Phillips, Ann Patricia. *The Prehistory of Europe.* Bloomington: Indiana University Press, 1980.

Rose, H.J. *A Handbook of Greek Mythology.* New York: Dutton, 1959.

Shepard, Paul, and Barry Sanders. *The Sacred Paw.* New York: Viking, 1985.

Thurston, Edgar. *Omens and Superstitions of Southern India.* New York: McBride, 1912.

White, T. H., trans. *Bestiary: A Book of Beasts.* New York: Putnam, 1954.

PERIODICALS

Barbeau, Marius. "Bear Mother." *Journal of American Folklore* 59 (January–March 1946): 1–12.

Breummer, Fred. "How Polar Bears Break the Ice." *Natural History* 93 (December 1984): 38.

Brody, Jane. "Boom in Poaching Threatens Bears Worldwide." *The New York Times* (May 1, 1990): C1.

Dobie, James Frank. "Juan Oso, Bear Nights in Mexico." *Southwest Review* 19 (April 1933): 34–64.

Flyger, Vagn, and Marjorie R. Townsend. "The Migration of Polar Bears." *Scientific American* 218 (February 1968): 108–116.

Hallowell, Irving A. "Bear Ceremonialism in the Northern Hemisphere." *American Anthropologist* 28 (January–March 1926): 1–75.

Lankford, G.E. "Pleistocene Animals in Folk Memory." *Journal of American Folklore* 93 (March 1980): 293–304.

National Audobon Society. *Audobon Wildlife Report.* San Diego: Academic Press, 1987.

Read, A.W. "Bear in American Speech." *American Speech* 10 (Spring 1935): 195–202

Speck, Frank G. "Penobscot Tales and Religious Beliefs." *Journal of American Folklore* 48 (January–March 1935): 1–108.

INDEX